Events on Cos, September 1943 -

Twenty days after the unjustifiable and monstrous violence of the German Gebirsjäger on the Acqui Division, a second offence was committed by the Grenadiers of General Müller's 22nd Division on Cos Island: 103 Italian officers were shot as Badoglio's troops and therefore considered traitors. Approximately one year after the tragic event, thanks to the will of some compatriots present on the island, 66 officers' bodies were found in eight mass graves. Only 42 were recognized. Today, their remains are at the Bari Overseas Military Ossuary. 37 officers were never found. The Italian Institutions did not want to search for them entrenching themselves behind the vastness of the area concerned. In 2015, with the Operation Lysias, a group of Italian volunteers and the indispensable contribution of some Greek friends, with limited economic and temporal means, did some excavation and found one common grave. Few bones and personal belongings other than some cartridges of the Grace Stroke were found. It is up to the Institution to complete the opera. This essay intends to tell what emerged from testimonies and archive documents with the aim of redeeming the memory and honour of those Men in arms.

Title: Events on Cos, September 1943 October 1945
Author: Pietro Giovanni Liuzzi
English revisor: John Cecil Fenton
Cover: Sophia Karajanni's photo
Cover Designer: Pietro Giovanni Liuzzi
ISBN: 978-88-92692-78-7
Youcanprint Self-Publishing
Via Roma, 73 - 73039 Tricase (LE) - Italy
www.youcanprint.it
info@youcanprint.it
Facebook: facebook.com/youcanprint.it
Twitter: twitter.com/youcanprintit

To Tea who knows everything about Cos,
Rebukes me for my many emotions,
Complains the long hours in solitude,
But she is proud of me.

to my friend Paul
Deus

Dec 2017

History must remember the victims
For what they suffered in the name of their homeland,
Even more if their death was unjust.

CONTENT

Introduction

When Aegean veterans speak of Coo [1], they use the term "small Kefalonia". The adjective is not related to the extension of the island but to the less number of Italian Army officers barbarously killed by the German soldiers in October 1943: 103 officers against 390 in Kefalonia. To the latter 3,800 soldiers must be added [2]. The motivation? Absurd: they were traitors. This is the reason why, even today, German Court expresses the verdict of non-punishment.

The barbarians who ordered or performed those homicides tried to hide the bodies of the Italians: in Kos they were buried in common ditches discovered almost a year later; in Kefalonia the bodies were thrown into the sea.

It is a debt of honour my commitment in carrying out this research to preserve the information and testimonies gathered so to keep alive their memory.

Arghiri Puglia is a Greek, Italian nationalized, who lives in our country since 1947. He left Cos together with his family for better living conditions. He spent in the island fourteen years: from 1930, when he was born, until 1944, when he fled from the German occupation. I was introduced to him by a common friend who knew of my interest in the 1943 war in Greece.

The encounter with Arghiri was, therefore, a lucky case because his memories, alive and intense, allowed me to deepen the knowledge of the Cos island, on the Dodecanese, giving to me a live account of those tragic moments of war which, quite often, return to him as a nightmare. Sometimes he was forced to break his story to overcome his emotion. *"Time cannot erase the memory"* he was saying, *"it can only dampen anger due to the impossibility of acting or reacting to such pain that terribly spread out on that island within few hours".*

---

[1] The text interchanges the names Coo, Kos and Cos.

2 G. Rochat, Essay on the Acqui in Kefalonia, in "Annali del Dipartimento di Storia", Università Tor Vergata, Roma, Dicembre 2006.

Arghiri was only the starting point amongst my contacts. After him I met other people associated to that part of the world which was an Overseas Italian Province for thirty years from where the Italians were sent away without their own belongings.

Having completed my first attempt in writing the story, I went to visit Cos Island to verify my work. Going around, after a few days, I felt like I had spent a lifetime over there. I passed through the buildings and imagined the life in those days. The Army Officer's Mess "Circolo Savoia", the sentry and the guard officer with the blue scarf at the entrance of the "Caserma Regina", the group of soldiers along the promenade and, then, the places of the killings. What a sadness!

Before talking of the tragic events which occurred to the Italian Army Officers, I believe it is advisable to mention some information on the Dodecanese Archipelago, on the island of Cos and the way of living during the Italian presence based on direct testimonies and reports stored in archives.

The search for living person reporting direct news on the massacre of the 103 Italian officers was in vain; however the availability of documents is such as to allow reconstruction of what happened from the 2nd to 7th October 1943.

THE DODECANESE AND COS ISLAND

The Dodecanese

The Dodecanese archipelago occupation was related to what was happening in the African Mediterranean area in 1911: France's intervention in Morocco worried the Italian government - fearing its expansion in that area and, therefore, in Libya. Italy had much interest on colonizing that region. Its interest grew in the years ahead.

At that time, the whole Africa Mediterranean region was a protectorate of Turkey, whose local authorities carried out incisive boycott actions to the penetration by Italian companies'. The Italian Prime Minister, Francesco Giolitti, without asking the Parliament's ratification and without informing the population, set up a military intervention force in order to secure an over-seas extension to Libya. The aim was to transfer the excess unemployed manpower there instead of to the United States as was already happening. On the contrary, failing such an opportunity would have reflected extremely negative consequences for Giolitti under pressure of rightist nationalist forces, banks and industrial groups: "*the fourth shore*" would have assured potential economic prospects.

So, in 1911, September 28th, an ultimatum was sent to Turkey to retire from that region in favour of Italy and, in a short time, on November 26th, a military expedition was organized. Public opinion was very surprised and, at the same time, divided among favourable and opposed to military intervention. The operations that followed were so quick and successful to silence those who opposed such an initiative. The situation, however, changed its course due to the contrast opposed by the guerrilla actions conducted by Libyan tribes. Although the Italian troops increased quite soon to 100,000 men they were forced to stop in the inhabited towns and in the deserted positions they conquered.

In order to encourage Turkey to abandon Libya, the Italian Government decided in April 1912 to move the war line front from the Mediterranean area to the Anatolian region. A naval squadron, commanded by Admiral Enrico Millo at first forced the Dardanelles

Strait to bomb the coastal fortifications and then occupied the Dodecanese in contravention of the directives imparted by the Government. The General, in fact, was ordered to take possession of the three major islands only: Rhodes, Leros and Cos.

In the period 6th to 20th of May 1912 the Italians, under the command of General Giovanni Ameglio, completed their goal: Calimnos, Leros, Patmos, Chalki, Stampalia, Nisiros, Scarpanto, Piscopi and Cos were occupied disarming the weak Ottoman garrisons. At last, Rhodes was conquered, a stronghold with a substantial Turkish military presence. Castelrosso, a tiny island of just 9 sq kms (69 mi south of Rhodes and just over 2 kms from Turkey), wanted to join Italy in 1920 as a free choice. During the military operations, the Italian forces were welcomed by the Greek population, markedly hostile to the 400 year Turkish occupation.

To the objections of the Austro-Hungarian government, Italy pledged to surrender the Aegean Islands immediately after Tripolitania and Cyrenaica had been freed of Turkish troops. The Ouchy Treaty of 18th October 1912 put an end to the war between Italy and Turkey, but Libya's guerrillas did not cease: Enver Pasha continued to resist, despite the troops who had abandoned the region. For retaliation, Italy kept the occupation of the Dodecanese. With the Treaty of Lausanne, signed on 24th July 1923, Turkey definitively lost its sovereignty over the Dodecanese in favor of Italy. This was done with the support of France and England to compensate Italy for its participation in World War I.

During the 35 years of Italian rule, the Dodecanese was an Italian province, named "Italian Aegean Islands", governed by a military administration until mid-September 1920.

The archipelago maximum development period began with the nomination of Mario Lago as governor, very much beloved by the islanders for his human and public qualities and for the commitment to modernize and improve their lives. His endeavours took place from 1922 to '36 and in that period were built roads, schools, hospitals, new agricultural villages and tourist facilities; the public education was stimulated and launched archaeological excavation campaign. The state of abandonment and poverty that came with Ottoman occupation soon ceased.

Governor Cesare Maria De Vecchi, took over from Mario Lago. He remained in office until 1940 contributing to the development of the Dodecanese but attempted to impose fascist culture on the islanders. He invested large amounts of Italian public money and that made at home harsh criticism; it was said that the capital poured into the improvement of the islands was superior to that available in the country.

«*The Regency of Mario Lago,* » says Renato Tringali, who lived many years in Rhodes and met both governors, « *was more incisive in the integration of local communities: Greek, Turkish, Jewish and of course the Italian*».

Supported by the educational work of the "Fratelli cristiani - Christian Brothers", Lago gave an ecumenical sign of great value to the population « *because he considered the four religions* » Tringali adds «*the Orthodox, the Muslim, the Jew and the Catholic, the sides of a Mountain on the top of it there is only one God* ».

This allowed free profession of faith, continuation of studies at their schools, where two hours a week Italian language was taught, leaving everyone an individual right to enroll and attend the courses at the Italian schools. Mario Lago, a great diplomat, was assisted in his action by his spouse who carried out social activities particularly in favour of people in need. For all these reasons, he was feared by the Greek "patriots" afraid of the Italianization of their people.

Lago appeared to the inhabitants of the Dodecanese as "the Italian" with characteristics of civilization, humanity and labour; De Vecchi, instead, was considered as the "*the Fascist*"; his personality was linked to the concept of oppression. To indicate the beginning of the De Vecchi's era, the islanders used to say "*when the fascists came*". He was unkind and bored enough to be hated by the people. In the headings of his letters he always featured all his titles: Count of Val Cismon - Quadrumviro della rivoluzione [1] - Governor of the Italian islands of

---

[1] He was one out of four to organize the Marcia su Roma in 1922, October 28th

LA DOMENICA DEL CORRIERE

	Si pubblica a Milano ogni Domenica	Uffici del giornale:
Anno . . . . . L. 8 – L. 10 –	Supplemento illustrato del "Corriere della Sera"	Via Solferino, N. 28
Semestre . . . . " 2,50 " 6 –		MILANO

Per tutti gli articoli e illustrazioni è riservata la proprietà artistica e letteraria, secondo le leggi e i trattati internazionali.

Anno XIV — Num. 21.   26 Maggio - 2 Giugno 1912.   Centesimi 10 il numero.

L'ultima vittoria : la guarnigione turca di Rodi, sconfitta con rilevanti perdite, si arrende e consegna le armi al gen. Ameglio.

(Disegno di A. Beltrame).

Achilles Beltrame, on the "La Domenica del Corriere", celebrates the victory of
General Ameglio on May 20, 1912 for the conquest of the Dodecanese
Archive Stamos J Papastamatiou

14

the Aegean. Gabriele D'Annunzio was able to define him « *the crashing idiot* » and «*the thundering nullity* ».

De Vecchi was replaced by General Ettore Bastico, in power until 1942, and then by Admiral Inigo Campioni, who kept the regency until he surrendered to the Germans in September 1943.

At that time life was quiet; the economic activities were thriving. The deep change took place in 1940, October 28, with the entry of Italy into a war against Greece. The situation created strong bitter moods in the Greek population who looked at Italy with admiration for its irredentism past. The critical time occurred in the Dodecanese when Italian citizens, expelled from Smyrna, arrived in the Dodecanese islands, where they practiced commercial activities, and, believing to ingratiate local fascist authorities, organized squad demonstrations. In Calimnos a lot of disorder were caused by a group of violent elements who brought in a procession a coffin wrapped in a Greek flag, leaping to the Duce and its interventionist politics. However the situation was taken under control and the protests immediately subsided. Some Greek families, considered to be opposed to the Fascist regime, were forced out of their homes. Obviously, at the right time, those families contributed to fueling square demonstrations and encouraging reactions against the Italians.

However, although the Greeks condemned the Italian aggression, their feelings against the Italians were not always marked by hate sentiments. For example, in a printed leaflet launched by the Greek *"Puri Cristiani – Real Christian"* soldiers at the beginning of their attack on the Italian troops, the solidarity for a people who were victims of the fascist dictatorship was reflected.

With the Dodecanese German occupation following the fall of the Fascism, the signing of the Italian-Anglo-American armistice and the British intervention in some islands, the rule of the region was exercised by General Ulrich Kleemann and then by Otto Wagener. The former was very preoccupied with the mass of Italian prisoners following the fighting because, if they were rebellious, they could have overcome the limited occupation troops.

It was Hitler, in order to remedy this danger, to send from Germany the staff to govern the merchant ships requisite in Aegean harbours to the Italians. Thus the transfer of prisoners from the islands to continental Greece and from there to Germany prison camps began.

It was a slaughter: **Donizetti** steamer, in September 23rd– 24th 1943, was sunk by two British destroyers, Eclipse and Fury; **Sinfra**, on October 18th of the same year, suffered an air attack and sunk; **Petrella**, was sunk by the British submarine Sportman on February 8th 1944, which departed from Suda, in Crete.

The ships carried, packed in their holds, a human burden of about 10,000 Italian prisoners, navigating to Piraeus; only 500 men were saved. **Oria**, former Norwegian Navy ship with the name Norda 4, having aboard 4,115 prisoners, while sailing towards Pireus was caught by a strong storm and ran aground near the island of Gaidaro (Agathonissi) where it broke in two sections. Only 27 men were saved.

[...] The horrifying wreckage, however, represents only a part of the many occurred in the Aegean Sea during the tragic odyssey of Italian prisoners [...] If the Germans are to be condemned for their barbaric ferocity [...] also the strategy of crashing freight loads of helpless people operated by the English Admiral must not be listed among the honourable war crimes committed by the belligerent allies. [...]

This was the outcry that Gino Manicone[2], veteran of concentration camps of Rhodes, wrote in his book "*Italians in Aegean.*"

General Kleemann tried to persuade Italian prisoners to enlist and fight with German troops; one of his very active collaborators was Captain Francesco Cerulli and his dedication was such that he deserved him, in a short time, advancement of rank on the field to major and then lieutenant colonel. Numerous prisoners also adhered to the request to avoid the suffering of the harsh imprisonment.

The assumption of command by General Wagener marked a critical period for the whole population, but even more for the Italian

---

[2] G. Manicone, *Italiani in Egeo*, Tipolitografia Abbazia Casamari, Frosinone, 1989, pp. 188-193.

prisoners who remained in the islands. He imposed a hellish regime on the prisoners, during which indelible actions were carried out reaching the culmination of homicidal madness.

When in May 9th, 1945 Germanic forces surrendered, General Wagener and his associates were subject to the judgment of the Military Tribunal in Rome. Wagener was sentenced to 15 years in prison for « *racing in violence with ill-treatment and murder by private Italian citizens* » and « *committing violence against Italian prisoners of war*». Other collaborators had lower penalties and others still excused from any accusation. The intervention of the Vatican and the pressure exerted by the German Chancellor Adenauer on the President of the Italian Council, Alcide De Gasperi, urged the Italian Republic President Luigi Einaudi to grant the grace.

Therefore, no one was imprisoned for the sentenced period. The Vatican's motivation strongly strides in comparison with the crimes committed in Rhodes by the "*Group of four*". In fact, the request stated: «*The Secretariat of State informs that Mrs. Wendula Wagener addressed the Holy Father asking for an interest in obtaining a measure of grace in favour of her husband, General Otto Wagener and four other Germans, sentenced by an Italian military court with penalties ranging from 9 to 15 years of imprisonment. It evocates that the convicts have children at an earlier age and are anxiously awaiting their own relatives, of which they are the only support* [3] ».

The news of German capitulation widened like spilt oil and aroused from the apathy the populations morally annihilated by the tyrannical yoke of occupants. The propaganda organized by Greek religious persons against the Italians in verbal form and leaflets, was supplemented by British liberators; this meant the hunting for the Italian colonizer, now a foreign usurper.

The repulsion for the Italians grew among the local population, especially young people, who didn't know what was done in the previous years to improve the islanders state of living: Greeks, Turks and Jews. The Fascist symbols were soon overthrown.

---

[3] F. Focardi, *Un accordo segreto tra Italia e Rft sui criminali di guerra. La liberazione del "gruppo di Rodi" 1948-1951*, in "Italia Contemporanea", 232, settembre 2003, hppt:/www.insmli.it/pubblicazioni/l/focardi232.pdf, 31/10/10, pagina 4 di 31.

In the interesting book *"The tragedy of Rhodes and the Aegean"*, Father Eduardo Fino, chaplain of the Italian Air Force in Rhodes, says that *"[...] began private vengeances. The Italian houses were marked with threatening, insults, crosses and Greek flags; [...] today, with the indulgent and pleasing eyes of the British, the Greeks set up a regime of terror against the Italians.[4] These were abused, reckless, beaten, robbed without mercy. The barracks were assaulted, the factories were devastated: [...] the Italians were driven out of jobs, employments, even from their shops and houses [...]. The British Command gave the order to not fraternize with the Italians [...]»*.

The peace treaty signed in Paris on February 10, 1947 forced Italy, a defeated nation, to convey to Greece its Aegean possessions. Article 14 imposes: (1) *the cession, in full, of the sovereignty on the Dodecanese Islands: Astypälea, Rhodes, Kharki, Kàrpathos, Kassos, Tilos, Nissyros, Kàlymnos, Leros, Patmos, Lipsi, Symi, Cos and Kastelòrizo, as well as adjacent islands;* (2) *their demilitarization and* (3) *allowed the British and Hellenic Governments to define the procedure and technical conditions to be implemented for the cession of the Dodecanese to Greece from whose territory the withdrawal of foreign troops should have taken place no more than 90 days after signing the treaty.*

On March 31st 1947, the British commander of liberation troops, General Geoffrey Parker, handed the Dodecanese to the Greek Admiral Periklis Joannidis. After a year, on March 7th 1948, the islands were definitively incorporated into the borders of Greece.

A condition of the treaty imposed the exclusion of every Italian citizen from the Aegean Islands, so in a few months, all abandoned their assets and returned to their homeland.

At a distance of years, the unmistakable memories come back to the forefront as the griefs are attenuating and not just from the Italian side only. Especially the elder inhabitants of those places, who lived the period of splendor of their islands, give value to what was brought about by work, culture, and intelligence of the Italian "colonizers" that contributed to the social improvement of those islands.

---

[4] E. Fino, *La tragedia di Rodi e dell'Egeo*, Assegeo, Milano, 1963, p. 288 e seguenti.

Cos island

The island of Cos is the third largest of the Southern Sporades after Rhodes and Karpatos. The surface, narrow, extends from E to W for 40 kms and has a maximum width of 11 kms. It is just 4 kms away from the west coast of Asia Minor and it is located at the entrance of a large inlet, Korfezi Gulf, bounded by the peninsulas of Halicarnassus to the north and Cnido (Resadiye) to the south. Bodrum is the nearest Turkish city.

Cos belongs to the Dodecanese administrative department.

The physical shape of the island is varied: steep, bare mountains with high peaks facing the sea, hills with rounded profiles, barren land and green plains. In particular, the Eastern part including Cos, the capital, is flat and is limited, on the south side, by a mountain range. It extends for three quarters of the length of the island, parallel to the coast; the highest peak is Mount Dikeos, which reaches 800 metres in height.

The central area of the island, Antimachia, is made up of a flat and uniform plateau, with an elevation of 100 to 300 metres above sea level, and streaked by numerous badlands. It narrows to the west.

The territory of Kefalos is a peninsula on the Western side of the isthmus: it is a harsh, mountainous, barren area. The highest peak is Mount Latra of 424 metres.

Cos is the Medicine Father's Birthplace, Hippocrates; it retains archaeological finds of classical, Hellenistic and Roman, times.

"*The island of the Blessed Ones*" was the ancient denomination of Cos since it was believed to be the residence of Gods and Heroes for its climatic characteristics: the summers, in fact, are refreshed by the Meltemi wind that lowers the high temperature, while winters are mild. Very often, though, there are marine storms that make navigation extremely difficult.

The ancient capital was Astipalea, today Kefalos, but the present one, which is named after the island, Cos, stands near a natural, shallow harbour, which is not suitable for ships. On one side of it stands the imposing castle built in 1315 by the Gerosolimitan Knights of St. John of Rhodes. They bought the island from the Venetians and ruled it for two hundred years when they were forced to abandon it following the Ottomans' continuous raids.

The economic activity carried out on the island by the Greek and Turkish communities was predominantly agricultural, while commerce was exercised by Jews who settled on the island after their expulsion from Spain at the end of 1400. The advent of the Italians caused a change of life.

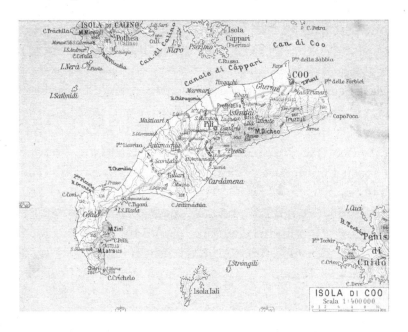

Cos island – L.V. Bertarelli, *Guida d'Italia del TCI, sez. Possedimenti e colonie*, Bertarelli, Milano, 1929 - Year VII, first edition

Italian workers, although considered invaders, were appreciated not only for their organization, but, above all, because of their ability, hard work and cooperativeness. Italian efficiency was governed by the *"Ordinamento fondiario - Land management"* that led to the establishment of the land registry. Topographical surveys were carried out in Cos between 1925 and 1931[5] and allowed the census of all properties, thus contributing to the elimination of disputes

---

[5] The Istituto Geografico Militare initial surveys of the island were carried out in 1925 and the first partial general survey in 1939

between families. In fact, until then, property rights were defined by words, according to the custom in use in the Ottoman Empire.

At that time particular attention was paid to the research and excavation of archaeological sites for the identification of traces of the Roman and Venetian domains.

Great benefits were brought to the island and to the Dodecanese as a whole by two state agencies: *the State Forestry Company and the Agriculture, Labour* and *Agricultural Experimentation Service.*

The area surrounding the capital was reclaimed marshes, cultivated with orchards and vineyards, and the new production technique applied to the fields is remembered with the anecdote of the onion. It is said, in fact, that in those years a bulb with extraordinary weight of a pound and a half was collected.

When a violent earthquake occurred on the island on April 23rd, 1933, two factors brought to light Italian sensitivity and ability to face disastrous situations: attention to the population and efficiency in reconstruction. In that circumstance, 150 people died and 600 others reported wounds. The Italian soldiers supported the population with impetus and generosity. The Cois were directed to the harbour and transported from there to the open countryside where they received garments and sustained with all kinds of comfort.

It is still acknowledged today that many houses with modern features were built and the properties assigned to families left with no home by the earthquake offering them the opportunity of repaying for the received benefit by very low and long repayment of rates.

The town had a different look at the end of the reconstruction activities: the roads, at first very narrow, were made larger; the houses had a different set of constructions, especially as far as the foundations were concerned. Until then a dried mixture of mud and straw was adopted; modern techniques and anti-seismic materials and criteria were used for the buildings.

Mostly appreciated was the construction of the sewage system that changed the hygienic state of the environment and people's way of life. Today the city still has that Italian architectural aspect: houses with gardens, rational and spacious public buildings, wide squares encircled by trees. The Aspa area, eastside of the town, and Kritika, to the West, were completely re-built with modern system; Hora was left as it was, and today, still untouched, receives many visitors either for its aspect and for its small, numerous, existing shops.

The social ethnic conflicts among Orthodox, Jewish and Muslim ceased during the Italian occupation. Manpower was fairly recompensed; welfare began to emerge since Mario Lago became Governor of the Dodecanese.

Unfortunately, things started to change with the declaration of war with Greece by the Italian government in 1940. The problems worsened with the arrival of the British troops in 1945 following the departure of the Germans. It was then that the Italians suffered all sorts of anger and the situation deteriorated with the arrival of the first troops of the Greek Army.

Ill-tempered, ill-treatment, ruthless hunt for Italians was made, so that much of the population was disgusted by their compatriots' behaviour. Many Cois hastened to conceal the hunted Italians in their homes. Moving from patriotic resentment to reaction for the Italian intervention against Greece, the Hellenic veterans returned to their island and tried to destroy the symbols of the Italian civilization. Even places of worship suffered damage.

The Agnus Dei Catholic Church, now a place of Orthodox worship, was flanked by a tall bell tower; it was knocked down by a cannon shell, creating a lot of resentment in the people who, in contrast, appreciated that example of fine workmanship.

Following the Dodecanese unification to the mainland, in 1947, the islanders and the Greeks in general knew a very difficult time due to war disasters and serious social crises which lasted for a decade (the Colonel regime era).

Many Cois emigrated in search of work and a better life in those years; they moved to Australia, the United States and Germany. However, over the years, many went back, longing for or having saved enough to afford a serene life at their home. Life in Cos had a positive turning point for tourism in the '70s, and it still represents the predominant activity in the island. Today very few islanders are engaged in agriculture.

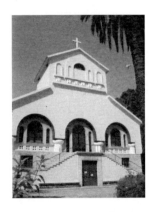

Prospect of the Church Agnus Dei as appeared before 1945 and the present aspect of the Church, now Orthodox without the bell tower

Dr. Giuseppe Gasparini, in a letter to the director of "*Il Giornale*" in February 1989, gives a testimony of esteem for Italians: *[...] even though the earthquake that struck the island of Cos in 1933 is not listed in official statistics, it is alive in the memory of the population especially due to what the Italians did in that circumstance [...]. In the square, below the Government palace, next to the famous Hippocrates plane twisted in its secular branches, I wanted to buy some postcards [...] then I asked an exile old lady behind the desk wondering how much I should have paid for my purchase. Speaking in Italian, with a smile, she said, "Allow me, Sir, to offer them to you. I never forget what the Italians taught me when I went to school in that palace down there and all the help they gave to our people during the terrible earthquake of 1933. "I will never forget those words and that gentle look so full of gratitude* [6] *[...].*

When an opinion is asked about the character of the three recent past island "dominators", the Cois are ready to connect the German to the British for the indifference they dealt with people, while the Italians, with the exception of the "*black shirts - fascists*", are generally judged with sympathy for their ability to fraternize. The Italian community in Cos was appreciated for their hard work commitment and ability to withstand it. Beyond the words, it is true that those

---

[6] Notiziario ARDE (Associazione reduci dell'Egeo), Anno XIX, N. 50, Marzo Aprile 1989, pag. 8.

peasants (the majority emigrated from Tuscany and Apulia) managed to understand and made productive a predominantly clay soil.

The German soldier is remembered as a robot; disciplined as a machine, but (at least as they used to appear) devoid of humanity; it was forbidden for them to fraternize with the local population and to have relations with Greek women for fear of harming their physical condition, as well as for personal security reasons. A disconcerting occurrence mentioned in Cos is that of a German soldier who grabbed by her shoulders a young woman draining water from a well. She screamed drawing attention of one of his superior officers. He rushed to the couple and, coldly, fired at the soldier killing him.

The British are characterized by abhorrence distinguishing the conqueror, but the islanders never forgot the huge amount of food that flowed into their land with their arrival. During the war period there was hunger and those who owned some supplies lived in terror of the German soldier's raids. The shortage of food, which in those years even mortified the occupation troops, forced the soldiers to search for it. None of the islanders had the courage to oppose food confiscation on the threat of death.

The arrival of the British liberators was greeted with great warmth because they brought freedom, but most feared they would settle permanently as it was happening in Cyprus. The bad thing was the imposition of their laws and coins marked with the British Military Administration (BMA), so that several times patriotic demonstrations were held to accelerate the absorption of the Dodecanese by Greece.

The gratitude of the islanders towards the Italians was clearly demonstrated during the fighting in Cos in October 1943 following the landing of German troops. Many Italian soldiers were helped to escape to Turkey or hidden in their homes to avoid them being captured.

The following images illustrate some of the buildings built in Cos during the Italian presence.

"Balilla House" now Bank   Museum   Metropolitan Bishop

"Fascism House" now Library   "Podestà Office" now Town Hall

"Podestà House" now Philarmonica (left)
"Savoia Officer Mess" now Avrà Bar [7] (right)

---

[7] The owner has restored the building as it was originally

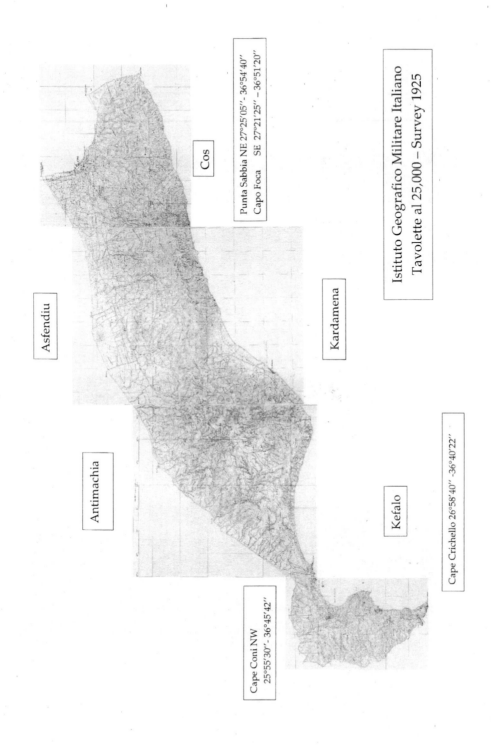

Asfendiu

Cos

Antimachia

Kardamena

Kefalo

Punta Sabbia NE 27°25'05'' - 36°54'40''
Capo Foca   SE 27°21'25'' – 36°51'20''

Istituto Geografico Militare Italiano
Tavolette al 25,000 – Survey 1925

Cape Crichello 26°58'40'' -36°40'22''

Cape Coni NW
25°55'30' - 36°45'42''

1943 GENERAL MILITARY SITUATION

The situation

The new Commanding officer of the Middle East Army, General Sir Henry Maitland, on the 16 February 1943, was entrusted with four main tasks by the Prime Minister, Winston Churchill:
- maintain the Eighth Army and support its operation to the utmost until Tunisia is finally cleared of the enemy;
- take all measures necessary for the mounting of that part of operation Husky to be launched from the area under his command;
- make preparations for supporting Turkey as may be necessary according to the policy of H. M. Government;
- prepare for amphibious operations in the Eastern Mediterranean.

On the **2nd of May 1943** the "Accolade" plan was ready, with the aim of the occupation of Rhodes and Scarphatos and, consequently, of all other Dodecanese islands.

To accomplish the plan the minimal requirement was:
- 3 infantry divisions,
- 1 armoured brigade
- 2 Independent infantry battalions
- 2 parachute battalions
- Corps troops
- adequate air cover.

The last constraint was due to the remoteness of the air bases in Egypt and Cyprus. It was hoped other large scale operations in the Mediterranean would deter the Germans from reinforcing the Aegean area.

Limitations on carrying out the plan were placed by General Eisenhower: "*any redeployment of British troops from North Africa to Middle East was subject to developments following operation Husky*".

On **12 May** Churchill proposed to the Americans the possibility that Turkey might offer air bases to reduce flying distance to hit oil fields in Romania and launch the attack on the Dodecanese.

The answer was negative. He insisted the primary aim of the Allied strategy was to proceed through Italy, prior to the attack through

France, and reach Berlin. Should Churchill insist on his idea the Americans threatened to concentrate their activities to the Pacific Theatre of War. Britain would have remained alone in the Mediterranean to fight Germany.

From **May to July 1943** Allied activities proceeded quickly:
- Sicily was occupied
- Forces were moving northwards
- Mussolini was ousted
- The Fascist era in Italy came to an end on the 25 July
- General Badoglio was the new Prime Minister
- The defeat of Italy was becoming a reality
- The Armistice between the new Italian regime and the Allies was being negotiated.

By **3 August,** the Accolade plan was ready. Then Middle East Forces Command requested:
- British air transport to lift a parachute battalion
- 4 squadrons of American P 38 Lightning aircraft

  Orders were given for:
- paratroops and aircrafts to be in position by 14 Aug
- Lightnings to be made available in Cyprus by the 15 Aug
- Seaborne troops made ready to sail at any time after the 18 Aug.

General Eisenhower was exasperated. It was his view that Accolade should have been abandoned since all men and materials were necessary for Italy.

The 8th Indian infantry Division assigned for Accolade was ordered to reach Italy and fight along the Adriatic coast.

Eisenhower was not happy, however Churchill was able to convince him that:
- there were reasonable prospect of success with the available forces;
- only when the activities in Italy would have allowed, Lighting aircraft could have been released.

Therefore Churchill decided to intervene in the Aegean venture. The Middle East Commanding Officer decided to assign to the Accolade operation the **234 Infantry Brigade** made up of:

- 1st Bn. The Durham Light Infantry;
- 2nd Bn. The Royal Irish Fusiliers;
- 2nd Bn. The Queen's Own Royal West Kent Regiment.

The success of the Accolade was dependent upon the
- Italian cooperation
- occupation of airfields in Rhodes
- amphibious landing feasible only if unopposed.

Thus a military mission was deemed necessary to pave the way for the main assault.

On the **9 September** Major Lord Jellicoe, Major Dolby, alias count Julian Dobrsky (a Polish Army officer) and Sergeant Keterston, a wireless operator, were parachuted into Rhodes to contact the Italian Dodecanese Governor Admiral, Igino Campioni.

At first Campioni was enthusiastic but his enthusiasm diminished knowing the British reinforcement units would have been only 200 men. The envoys were ordered to leave the island.

On **11 September** Colonel L.F.R. Kenyon and Group Captain Harry Wheeler carried out a second attempt but with no better results. Admiral Campioni surrendered. Rhodes was conquered by the Germans without fighting. 35 to 40,000 men were taken prisoner by 7,000 invaders.

Revision of the plan was then necessary. Operational plans were altered to refer only to Cos, Leros and Samos. In particular Cos was considered an indispensable base for single-engined fighters in order to :
- provide short range cover for a proposed landing at Rhodes scheduled late October 1943;
- protect British warships operating out of Leros.

By **middle September 1943** the following was available:
- 22 DC3 Douglas Dakotas (8 were paratroop aircraft),
- 120 men of A Coy 11th Bn. "The Parachute Regiment".

14 Sept:
- 1 Beaufighter landed on Antimachia airdrome and offloaded a wireless team;

- Beaufighters and Dakotas continued all day, going to and from between Nicosia (Cyprus) and Antimachia (Cos) to transport men and material, flying along the Turkish coast avoiding being intercepted by the German surveillance; the duration of the flight: 3 hours, the first destined to take off at 22.41 hours.

14 Sept:

- Lieutenant Colonel R.F.Kirby of 1st Battalion DLI landed at Cos with advance elements of his command;
- Colonel Kenyon appointed CO of the troops on Cos.

15 Sept:

- paratroopers and DLI had been joined by
- Army gunners (40 mm Bofors still enroute by sea)
- a detachment of 2909 Squadron RAF Regiment with 20 mm Hispano cannon
- RAF signallers and radar technicians plus ground crews
- pilots of the 7 Squadron equipped with Spitfire MkV's.

By the same date the German had been alerted to the presence of British Forces on Cos; in consequence, intense, heavy bombing operations began with Me 109's hitting Antimachia Airfield, several Dakotas being destroyed. Also the runway suffered heavy damage.

Italian Units in Cos

On Cos there were 3,500 – 4,000 Italians comprising the majority of 2nd and 3rd Battalion of the 10th Infantry Regiment "Regina" with heavy weapons including:

- 1 company of 81 mm mortars
- 1 company of gun 47/32
- 252nd antitank company
- 10th coastal machine gun company

- 24th coastal machine gun company
- 403rd ex "Black shirts - Fascists" machine gun company
- XXXI artillery group (3 batteries = 2 of 75/27 and 1 of 149/12)
- LXXXII antiaircraft group (3 batteries = 62nd, 63rd, 64th of 75/27 A.V.)
- 136th battery
- 295th machine gun battery (armed with 20 mm cannon)
- various support units

British Units in Cos

Air Defence: consisting of a small group of Spitfires (South African). Air Force personnel: around 500 officers and men, divided between 2901 and 2909 Squadrons of the RAF Regiments at Antimachia and Lambi (NE of the island – Cape Sabbia).

Army Personnel:
- 76 officers and men of 4 Batteries Light AA Regiment Royal Artillery, total 680
- 540 men all ranks of the DLI

DLI Deployment :
- Companies A, B, HQ of the Battalion in the area stretching from the northern coast to SE for nearly 2 kms up to within 800 m of Ghermé (Platani)
- Company C allocated in Cos town
- Anti-tank Platoon at Lambi landing ground
- Company D plus 2 detachments of the Mortar Platoon and 1 section of Carrier Platoon at Antimachia airport.
- Antiaircraft armament distributed at Antimachia and around Cos town: 25 40 mm Bofors and 24 20 mm Hispanos

German's Activities before the attack

23 September

General Friedrich Wilhelm Müller, Commanding Officer 22nd Infantry Division was ordered by the Army Group E in Athens, to prepare sufficient units to attack and conquer Cos and Leros.

Cos was given a greater priority than Leros for its important air bases.

Müller's plan was based exclusively on surprise with three units:
- 1 Battle Group to land on Marmari beach, on the north of the island; the task was to land on the coast and then split in 2 branches: one aiming for Cos town and the second for Antimachia Airport.
- 1 Battalion to land below point 428 (Mount Eremita), on the south coastline, at the foot of a steep terrain. The task was to destroy Italian gun emplacements south of Platani and to cover Cos and its port.
- 1 joint amphibious / air landing unit to land on the west side of the island at Cape Tigani. Its task was to neutralize Antimachia airport and eliminate any resistance in the West of the island.

The compositions of the units were:
  - Commanding Officer and his Staff
  - Von Saldern Battle Group, named for its Major Commanding Officer, made of:
    - II Battalion/ Grenadier Regiment 65
    - III Battalion/Grenadier Regiment 440
    - 3rd and 4th Battery/Artillery Regiment 22
    - 3rd Battery/AA Battalion 22
    - 2nd Company/Pioneer Battalion 22 less 1 platoon
  - Aschoff Battalion, named for its Captain Commanding Officer, made of:

- II Battalion/Grenadier Regiment 16 (utilizing only mules)

- <u>Joint Unit</u>, made of

- 15th Company /Regiment Brandenburg 4, Commanding Officer Lieutenant Oschovitz

- 1st Company / Kustenjäger Abteil Brandenburg, Commanding Officer Captain Armin Kulhmann

<u>Transport arrangements</u> were reliant on:

- 5 steamships: Trapani, Schiaffino, Città di Ravenna, Kari, Ingeborg

- 9 landing-craft

- 3 pioneer-boats

- 2 escort vessels

- Minelayers

- 5 corvettes

- 4 coastal defence vessels

- 3 mine sweepers

THE BATTLE

Chronological Activities

1 October - Morning
The German assault troops gathered
- at Heraklion, Crete: the Commanding Officer, the Battle Group Staff Officers and the II Battalion/Grenadier Regiment 16
-   at Suda, Crete: the II Battalion/Grenadier Regiment 65, the 3rd and 4^{th}Battery/Artillery Regiment 22, the 3rd Battery/AA Battalion 22, the 2^{nd}Company/Pioneer Battalion 22 less 1 platoon
-   at Athens – Piraeus : the III Battalion/Grenadier Regiment 440 and the 15th Company /4 Regiment Brandenburg
-   at Tatoi Airport – Athens : the 1st Company / Küstenjäger Abteil Brandenburg

1 October - Evening
Embarkation completed

Departure

2 October - Morning
Rendezvous in the Cyclades

Landing exercise by landing craft personnel

2 October - Afternoon
The convoy splits in two sections as a deception: one heading to Rhodes (SE) and the other to Ikaria island (NE)

Force 292 (the Accolade Operational Command in Cairo) received a signal stating during the afternoon a convoy including three transport vessels had been reported steering South to Naxos. It was assumed the convoy was heading to Rhodes (already occupied by the Germans)

2 October - Evening
The two sections changed direction sailing toward Cos and stopped between Pserimos and Kalimnos

2 October - <u>Night</u>

A squall, resulting in a rough sea, threatened to jeopardize the operation.

Later the squall relented and the sea became smooth.

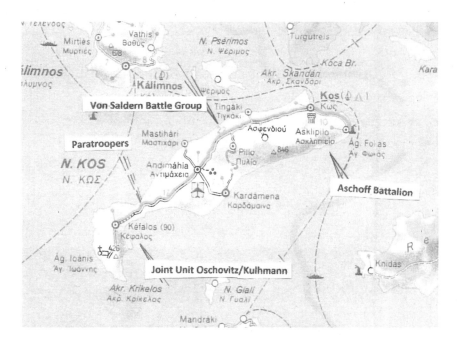

Directions of German attack

German-British Activities

3 October - Early morning

Captain Blagden, of the British Operational Command in Cos, was alerted by the RAF HQ at Antimachia of the presence of a convoy Heading Eastwards, at 11.20 on the previous day, approximately 12 miles South of Melos Island.

A few minutes later Captain Floccia, the Italian Officer on duty at the Italian Command Post, asked his British opposite number if a convoy was expected. Days before, British ships, sometimes, arrived unexpectedly.

The captain decided to inform Colonel Kenyon, the British Commanding Officer. He misinterpreted the information on the convoys; in fact he believed the convoy was going to Rhodes. He didn't take any action.

Because of the alarming information arriving with increasing intensity, Colonel Kenyon and Colonel Felice Leggio, the Italian Commander, decided to ascertain the actual situation. When, eventually, the alarm was given to the troops on the island, it was too late. The Germans had a foothold on Cos.

The first waves of German troops were of the II Battalion/Grenadier Regiment 65. They took possession of the beachhead and as soon as other troops arrived, they moved along the coast to reach Tingaki airstrip. South African Pilots and ground crew fled to Cos town and from there to Turkey, leaving 6 Spitfires to the enemy.

The Italian units along the coast were overrun by the speedy advance of the Germans.

In the absence of Lieutenant Colonel R.F. Kirby, Commanding Officer of the DLI, who was in hospital, his second in command, Major Hugh Vaux, alerted companies A and B and dispatched a Carrier Platoon to Marmari area for reconnaissance. After a while, an NCO returned reporting the enemy forces had engaged the platoon and, to avoid being overrun, it broke contact and withdrew to the main Antimachia - Cos road.

At 0610 the British units were ordered to take position as follow:
- B Coy: astride the main road West Platani
- HQ Coy: to cover the ground between B Coy and the coast
- A Coy: in reserve at Andisli region between Ingurlichi and Cos
- C Coy: in reserve in Cos. Later, following erroneous information about enemy landings at Cape Foca, on the eastern coast of Cos, the Company received orders to take position and defend that area

- HQ Bn. in an olive grove NW of Platani.

At 0900 3rd Battalion/Grenadier Regiment 440 began to arrive giving the 2nd Battalion/Grenadier Regiment 65 the opportunity to proceed forward in an Eastern direction to reach Cos town. The Germans silenced each gun battery along the way.

A Coy was invested by the German's attack and later it was the turn of B Coy and HQ Coy. The attack was supported by violent air attacks and heavy shelling.

Lt Col. Kirby, discharged himself from the hospital, and, following a quick survey, he gave orders to:

- A Coy to move 1200 mts SW to strengthen the line held by B Coy;
- HQ Coy to stay along the Dermen Valley;
- D Coy in Antimachia could not be contacted and remained out of control.

Following heavy bombardment and infantry attack, A Coy was pushed back 800 mts nearer Platani with an estimated loss of 50% casualties. A joint defence was implemented with A Company and the 5th Company of the 10th Regiment.

Then it was the turn of B Coy and HQ Coy to come up against the II./Grenadier Regiment 65.

To maintain position Lieutenant Colonel Kirby ordered the transfer of 30 men of the Anti-Tank Platoon based in Lambi to reinforce the sector held by A and B Companies;

From Lambi 4 Bofors guns opened fire on the Germans in front of A and B Company sectors.

Between 12.00 and 14.00 2 platoons of B Coy were overrun and Captain Stafford, ordered the unit to withdraw up the line held by HQ Battalion. Major Vaux gave a similar order to the HQ Coy.

At 17.15 Lieutenant Colonel Kirby issued orders to pull back and form a defence line around Cos. A Coy didn't receive the order and remained in position.

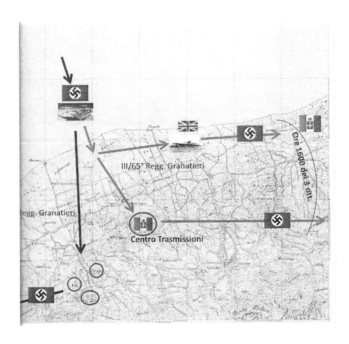

Eastward German attack

The Germans advanced up to a line from Platani, SE to the town outskirt and NE to the coast at Lambi. From then the situation was becoming difficult for the defenders and four options had to be considered by the Commanding Officer:

- defend their position to the last man
- fall back on Cos and conduct a final withdrawal along the coastal corridor as far as Cape Foca (SE)
- take to the hills to conduct guerrilla action
- surrender.

The decision was to leave under cover of darkness for Turkish waters. The departure was delayed till half an hour after dusk.

Flying Officer B.W. Purcell's impression was that "...*it look like a general evacuation...Men were trying to paddle out on doors, pieces of wood, etc..... I tried it myself and found it impossible.*" Eventually Purcell reached Turkey by swimming.

At 19.00 Lieutenant Colonel Kirby asked for a Senior Officer's Meeting in Cos near Paleologou Square. Five officers gathered for briefing when a mortar bomb exploded next to them. Three officers were badly injured: Major Leather, Captain Stafford and Captain Bush. They were later taken prisoner.

Major Vaux meanwhile resumed command and was told by Colonel Kenyon to prepare for the arrival of British paratroopers and an infantry battalion. It was false information. From then the transfer of the British started using all types of boats. Some soldiers went up to the hills to hide from the Germans hoping eventually to be transferred to Turkey.

German-Italian Activities at Mount Eremita

3 October - Morning

By 0800 all German units landed on the South coast of Cos. At first the 5th and the 8th company arrived and then the 6th, the 7th and two Pioneer Platoons.

They started immediately to take over Point 428 (Mount Eremita); progress was not easy because the terrain was difficult and slowed them down. When they reached the top they had an impressive view of the plain. Their objective was at 2 kms distance.

The Commanding Officer, captain Aschoff, assessed the situation and established the formation of its units:
- 6th Company on the front
- 5th Company to cover the right side of the 6th
- 7th Company to cover the left side of the 6th
- 8th Company in reserve.

The force started toward their objectives on the plain.

The troops suffered casualties due to the Italian fire, which was accurate. They rushed from one position to another.

It took 2 hours to come near the Italian position: the 7th joined the 6th. The 5th were separated from the others because of enemy strong points.

The 1st Pioneer Platoon was tasked to spearhead the Italian position next to Asklepion where it was supposed there was the presence of an ammunition dump.

At 1350 the attack began under strong enemy fire and finally a gap in the defence perimeter was found. Near Asklepion the three companies faced tough resistance whilst the 8th reached the Italian battery near Platani.

Although the air attack was violent, the undeterred defender unit continued to keep the enemy at a distance.

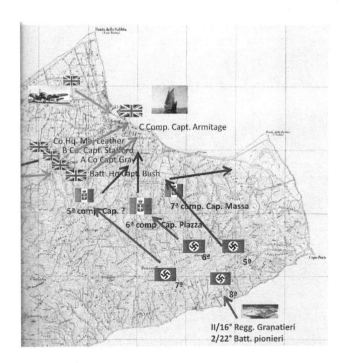

German attack from South East

45

Major Vaux stated: *two Italian companies on the left of A Company were engaged by the enemy coming down from the hills and were fighting well and, in fact, held those position until dusk although there was some enemy infiltration on their left flank.* (PRO: WO 106/3146) {The two Italian companies were the 6th and the 5th}.

Shortly before nightfall a new German attack was launched. Only at about midnight, following heavy mortar bombing and taking heavy casualties the German launched a fresh attack.

The defenders had, in the meantime, left the position. The Germans, taking full advantage of this unexpected situation, inflicted heavy losses among the fleeing troops.

Late in the night the German units overran all the Italian positions and they stopped at the outskirts of Cos town.

German-Italian Activities at the Salt plain (Salina)

3 October

At 0900 the III Battalion/Grenadier Regiment 440 landed.

At 1000 General Müller and his staff landed on Tingachi beach and directly took full control of the situation.

The Italian Artillery started to shell the ships off Pserimos and Kalimnos. The German vessels were forced to move behind those two islands causing delays in trans-shipping materiel and the servicing crews.

Rapidly, without any effective resistance by the Italians, the Unit reached a line defined by Lacu (point 66) and Profeta Elia (point 211) where the Italian Tactical Command Post was situated.

By 1300, having occupied Pili, Saint Nicolas and Saint George, General Müller ordered the unit to move towards Antimachia airport to join the units landed at Cape Tigani.

The movement was without difficulty up to Kefalo where there was located Lieutenant De Giovanni and his company, the 12th. Here the Germans found tough resistance. The Commanding Officer of the German Unit stopped his troops for the night, but he ordered Captain Squeo, Commanding Officer of the 136th Artillery Battery, who had been taken prisoner, to approach De Giovanni in his emplacement to convince him to stop fighting. Twice Captain Squeo was sent on this mission, and each time he was rebuffed. De Giovanni knew, from radio communications from Lero, Cyprus and Alexandria, that reinforcements and supplies were meant to be arriving the next day, which would help him maintain his position.

German-Italian-British Activities at Antimachia

3 October

Due to rough seas, Captain Kullmann arrived late at Tigani Beach therefore he was unable to secure the Coscinari landing area for the paratroopers. They arrived at 0700 and suffered heavy losses while descending. The Italian defence in that area was efficient.

At 0840 the two German units linked up and repulsed an Italian attack from the West.

A group of paratroopers were directed against the enemy whilst the mass of the Germans was prepared to attack along the road, which goes to Antimachia.

The unit proceeded under heavy Italian artillery fire but the advance was strong enough to overrun infantry units and gun positions. They stopped at a line 3.5 kms from Antimachia Airport.

At this line they paused for ammunition supply. The Italian captured soldiers were used as porters.

Schnellboat - Fast attack boat: 33 m long, 5 m wide; excellent sailing of the sea. Two launchers and four torpedoes supplied; three 20mm cannons, one 37mm. and machine guns. Speed 43 knots.

Source: Imperial War Museum, London

At the airport, Captain Thorpe, Commanding Officer of D Coy, was unable to contact by wireless or land line the HQ Battalion. He dispatched a messenger by motorcycle but he was killed en route.

At 1400 the German movement started again. An Italian battery surrendered: the 52ª Battery Commanding Officer hoisted a German Flag. His name was Captain Nasca, a fascist. It was he who personally fired a few rounds of gunfire against Antimachia airport. At the end of the war he was condemned for treason.

At 1730 Captain Thorpe, considering the high risk of the situation, ordered his adjutant to destroy all documents and for his unit to retreat to the Stefanena Valley, South of the Airport, towards Kardamena.

The Captain was injured during the second German air attack on the airport. He got first aid in a Greek house, eventually being taken prisoner by the Germans.

At 1810 the Germans secured the airport. Thirty British were captured.

Captain Clark of MI14 supervised the departure from Kardamena of several boatloads of evacuees.

4 October
Central and East area of Cos Island

Early in the morning German air attack started again. Sustained by artillery fire, the II Battalion/Grenadier Regiment 65 and the II Battalion/Grenadier Regiment 16 launched the assault to secure Cos town, Lambi airstrip and then the SE area up to Cape Foca.

The advance was relatively easy because of the lack of resistance.

Antimachia and West area of Cos island

The German attack started quite early; air attacks were numerous and efficient. The fighting to conquer Kefalo, the position held by Lieutenant De Giovanni, resisted until 1400. By that hour Cos Island was conquered.

Air Force Activities

The Luftwaffe carried out their job with great efficiency and their superiority was indisputable; fighters and transport carriers operated with impunity.

What veterans remember is the terrible shriek of the sirens of the Stuka when diving, designed to create panic and fear in the troops

The Italian Forces consisted of seven fighters, but only one pilot was available, Lieutenant Morganti. He did manage to intercept a

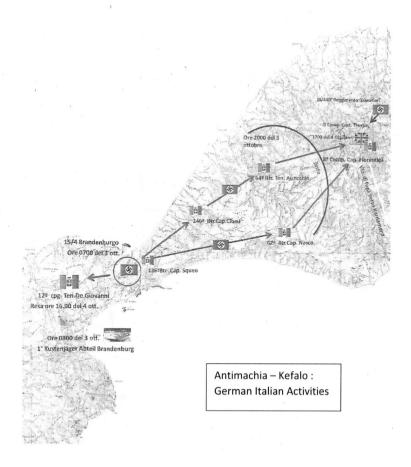

Antimachia – Kefalo :
German Italian Activities

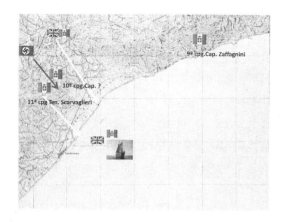

Escape routes

squadron of bombers flying from Rhodes to Athens and shot one down, returning to Antimachia unscathed.

Dakota transport did a magnificent job of transporting men and material. When Antimachia airport was bombed they operated on Lambi airstrip, mostly flying at night. When that too was destroyed they supplied by parachute drops

In Antimachia there were South African Air Force' Spitfires and Beaufighters. When the first group of Spitfires were destroyed on the ground by the German aircraft, they were replaced by the same SAAF on the airstrip near Tingaki.

The pilots did their utmost, and fought desperately but German air supremacy did not allow too much flexibility.

Lieutenant Colonel R.F.Kirby CO 1st DLI Battalion
Captain John H Thorpe CO DLI D Company

Major Hugh Vaux Vice C O 1st DLI Battalion
Major K.M.W. Leather C O HQ Bn 1st DLI Battalion
By courtesy of
Durham County Record Office, Londonderry Estate Archives, D/Lo/C113

Supermarine Spitfire, single-seater, low-wing, single-engine fighter airplane. Speed 594 km/h, range 1827 kms. Four 7.7 mm machine guns, two 20mm cannons, two 113kg bombs.

Junker JU-87 Stuka, two-seater, single-engine, diver bomber. Equipped with a siren that came into operation in diving attacks. Speed 410 km/h at 3.840 m. in altitude. Three 7.92 mm machine guns and bombs for 1800 kg. Range 1.535 kms.

Macchi M.C. 202 Folgore, fighter, single-seater, single-engine. 596 km/h at 599 m. elevation. Fuel distance 765 kms. Two Breda 12.7 mm machine guns with 400 cartridges per weapon. Two 7.7mm machineguns with 500 shots per weapon.

Images from Blogger "Soldado del mundo"

ARCHIVAL REFERRALS

The "**Actors**" are listed below with the document references

Aiello	A.U.S.S.M.E.[8] 2129/B/4/8
Anselmi/Costa	A.U.S.S.M.E. 2129/B – 05835/18.12.45 e 1099/ 18.3.46
Bacheca	A.U.S.S.M.E. 2129/B/4/11
Coridali	A.U.S.S.M.E. 2129/B/
De Prosperis	Interview / Pagoaki (Cos) Interview
Esposito	A.U.S.S.M.E. 2129/B/1/18 n. 415 del 4. 2. 1946
Floccia	A.U.S.S.M.E. 2129/B/
Gianazzi	A.U.S.S.M.E. 2129/B/ 10266 del 5.12 1945
Mondini	A.U.S.S.M.E. 2129/B/4/11 - 2205/ST del 2.6.46
Nasca	A.U.S.S.M.E. 2129/B/4/2 2294 del 22.6.46 e 1186 del 4.4.46
Orlando	A.U.S.S.M.E. 2129/B/1/12 9209 del 8.11.1945
Poggiani	Private correspondence
Puglia	Interview
Santini	A.U.S.S.M.E. 2129/B
Squeo	A.U.S.S.M.E. 2129/B/
Taberini	A.U.S.S.M.E. 2129/B/ "Il Reduce" newspaper, Dec. 45
Ignoto	Durham County Records Office Londonderry Estate Archives, D/Lo/C113
Zucchelli	Comando Generale Arma Carabinieri - Archivio Storico

---

[8] A.U.S.S.M.E : Archivio Ufficio Storico Stato Maggiore Esercito

THE BATTLE TOLD BY THE ACTORS

Cos Sector – Italian activities

(Orlando) [9] *The news that Italy asked and obtained an armistice came to Cos on the evening of the 8 September 1943, with the newsreel broadcast at 2000.*

Two days after the armistice, an allied airplane flew over the island at about 1900 and launched some parachutes which were later collected by us. With them were launched packs and cylinders. It was not possible to trace the paratroopers who, deprived of all the material, came to the Military Command of the island the following morning.

The parcels contained a radio and food supplies. The paratroopers, a captain and a sergeant, both British, were received by Colonel Felice Leggio, and after an interview, they were escorted to a cottage to await the Italian decision.

On the evening of the same day, the Italian Commander informed the British that he fully adhered to the proposal of the allied forces cooperation and invited them to pass on his decision to their command in Cairo. A few days later, a motorboat arrived in Cos Harbour, carrying a colonel, various other officers, and 30/40 privates.

At the meeting immediately held between the two colonels, Italian and English, at the regiment command office, two more persons were in attendance: a senior Italian officer and an English liaison officer. A collaboration agreement was reached as a result of the discussion.

The initial crew who arrived by boat was reinforced some days later by about 100 paratroopers descended on to the island. The aviation field was handed to the RAF where soon some Spitfires landed.

Lieutenant General Desmond Anderson, an English general, inspected the island and arranged for the arrival of supplies and reinforcements. In fact, a few days later, two light infantry companies, about 200 men, and 40 mm anti-aircraft guns to defend the harbour and Antimachia landing arrived.

The German air attacks began whilst activities to improve defensive

---

[9] Regiment Staff Office, Captain

arrangements of the island were underway in connection with the new situation, including planning the construction of two other landing fields, one near Punta Sabbia at Lambi, NE of Cos, and the other on the Kardamena plain, SW of the island. Luftwaffe raids heavily continued before and after their landing took place.

At dawn on 3 October 1943, after a long lasting air bombing at night, watchmen at Linopoti reported that some landing boats were approaching the coast. The Navy observation station at Cape Foca, SE of the island, gave the alarm on other approaching boats.

The 2ⁿᵈ battalion was deployed next to the ammunition depot at Ambavri to oppose and eventually eliminate the German troops who landed next to the Spa, at the Southern slope of the hills between Calchipetra and Allatti. Italian defensive installation in that area had already prevailed and the Germans were now facing Ambavri's hilltop position.

Radio contact with the 3ʳᵈ battalion in Antimachia sector was impossible.

The Germans troops, landed at various spots on the island, and paratroopers, descended in the vicinity of the artillery batteries positions, broke the whole defensive system. Only one unit, the 12ᵗʰ Machine Gun Company, under command of Lieutenant De Giovanni, was organized as a strongpoint on the other side of the isthmus, at Kefalo. He maintained his position for about two days against German attacks exerted by infantrymen, paratroopers and armoured vehicles with 81 mm mortar.

In the Ambavri area, during the fight, the rifle company commanded by Lieutenant Piazza was distinguished. He kept the assigned position throughout day 3 and the following night, causing heavy losses to German troops. In the meantime, other Italian units had to move from Ambavri in an area between the town and Cape Foca. However, overwhelmed by the German forces and unable to oppose the attacks of the German planes who bombed and machine gunned Italian troops and positions, at 09.30 on October 4, 1943 they were asked the surrender.

(De Prosperis) [10] [11] *I was on guard the night from October 2 to 3, 1943. I heard increasingly noises far from the coastline. I had no doubt about the noises that came from the sea, overlooking the north coast. During the night noise spreads distinctly and fast, so I felt that someone was carrying out military service operations.*

Alarmed, I rushed from my machine gun position to the barracks. I opened the officer's door and told him loudly: "The Germans are landing!" Lieutenant D'Amore tried to calm me: "No, the British are carrying other material for the defence of the island."

Then I returned to my place a little shaken. My commanding officer should have made sure himself before answering that way! Even today, thinking back, I do not consider him guilty for that reaction. He was in bed feverish. Moreover, the Regimental Command, on the basis of the British information, was certain that the Germans would only attack the island with paratroopers and not with landing boats.

Suddenly, I heard shooting along the coast of Tingaki, where the noises came from. I went back to the house, called the alarm, and, along with two other comrades, took a Breda machine gun, a box of ammunition, and returned to my place.

It did not take too long. Three German armoured vehicles appeared shortly in front of me. I recognized them from the swastika. I started shooting and spent all ammunition. The barrel had become glowing and I had to change it. I needed another ammunition box, but I realized I was left alone.

Meanwhile, a sidecar-motorcycle with three armed German soldiers appeared on the road in front of me. I decided to run away to avoid capture. It was 0730; the Germans had already penetrated deeply into the Tingaki - Linopoti area reaching the main road Cos Kefalo.

---

[10] De Prosperis Severino, class 1923, born in Fiuggi, from October 27, 1942 to September 8, 1943 participated in war operations in the Aegean with the 10th Regiment Infantry "Regina". Prisoner of war until May 8, 1945. When returned to Italy he was sent on leave for good. In the document handed to him there were the following sentence *"no charges can be raised on the circumstances of the capture and the conduct held as a prisoner"*. In 2016 he obtained the Medaglia della Liberazione - The Medal for the Freedom - at pag.159

[11] *The memory of a machine gunner* at pag. 154

I headed to Pilì, direct to Mount Dicheo hoping for salvation. Being just twenty years of age and the fear of being caught by the enemy allowed me to sustain an effort I was not used to.

(Floccia) [12] *Relations among the Italian and the English commander, officers and troops, day by day became ever closer such as to exchange mutual greeting.*

The first, quite heavy, German airstrike happened on 27 September. Several bombs fell on Cos town. Air duels took place in the sky and numerous losses were counted on both sides. Antimachia Airport was hit several times and, as a retaliation, Rhodes airport (already in German hands) was bombed by English airplanes.

In one day, 13 British transport planes and some fighters were destroyed on the ground. The German preparation for the attack on the island became more and more obvious and validated the hypothesis that it could come from the sky. In fact, on September 25, Captain Saxton, an English liaison officer, told the Italian Command that about 200 German airplanes had been detached from the Russian front to an airfield near Athens according to the British Intelligence Service.

On the night of 2 to 3 October 1943, I was on duty at the Island's Command.

At 0310, Lieutenant Lorusso, commanding a machine gun platoon at Monte Eremita, phoned to inform the headquarters his observers had spotted light beams at sea from Turkey towards Cape Crio. These reports were passed several times for months so that at the Island's Command they no longer bothered them.

However, the order for maximum vigilance was given to all watchers.

At 0315 Lieutenant Coratza, commander of the 81 mm mortar platoon at Linopoti, asked by phone whether some motorboats approaching Marmaris and Masticari beaches were Italian or English.

---

[12] Regiment Staff Office, Captain

On the previous evening, October 2, it had been reported to all units on the island that, starting from 2145 at every forty-five minutes, allied planes would fly over the island and drop supplies and on the following morning, at 0500, October 3, an Italian tanker, Nero, would arrive at Cos.

No motorboats arrival were foreseen. Colonel Leggio was alerted by phone and he ordered the English command be asked for information. In the negative case, he gave the instruction to open fire against the boats.

This order had already been given in advance to Lieutenant Coratza.

Coratza called again to say that the machine gun fire from the watch stations along the coastline had been answered by firing from the motorboats. This gave certainty that they were facing the enemy. I got in touch with the Marmaris squad, the one who started firing. I heard: "Here they are, they are with us". The phone operator shouted like an assaulted person. Then, the conversation abruptly stopped.

This confirms the landing in Linopoti area took place at 0330 on 3 October 1943.

At the same time, confusing, alarming, frustrating reports relating to enemy troops landing at various sectors of the coastline overwhelmed the Command switchboard.

The roar of the plane engines, which began at 2115 on the 2 October lasted all night. There was no clear difference from the passage of British planes or the Germans ones. These were recognized only when bombing started on the city and its surroundings.

The first crisis among the units occurred at the first air bombing. The orders given by the Italian and English Command on 27 September were that, in case of air strike, the troops encamped on the outskirts of the city had to escape to different shelters and trenches from their emplacements.

So, at the time of the landing the troops were scattered throughout the countryside in their shelters.

The switchboard operator had no chance to listen to all calls coming from all over the island. Each one referred to urgent news.

"The switchboard incoming call lights are all on. Who should I consider first?" the excited operator was crying.

It made clear that all the units on the island were aware of the beginning of the landing. Colonel Leggio immediately arrived by car at the Regiment Command to ascertain the magnitude of the situation. Captain Colussi Giovanbattista gave him the briefing

Meanwhile, several dozen aircraft were flying over the city and neighbouring areas.

Colonel Leggio, along with Captain Colussi, decided to transfer his command post to the Ambavri area where the telephone switchboard was located and gave me the order to remain at the office until I received new orders. At 0600, the barracks was machine-gunned by Stuka. Shortly after the bombing in the surrounding area, I moved with the secret coded documents to the Ambavri Tactical Command.

At 0700 the situation was as a such:

-   enemy landed at Cape Foca and on the slopes of Mount Eremita. After climbing the hills he came down to the valley to attack the town

-   the 7th Company deployed on the left, the 6th in the middle, the Autonomous Unit reinforced by the Cannon Company platoons and a mortar platoon on the right wing;

-   the 8th Company in support at the rear.

-   at about 0530, the 75/27mm and the 65/17mm batteries at Ghermè area, next to Ambavri, started firing on Mount Eremita against the first German contingent moving downhill.

- at 0700 Captain Oliviero Giovanni of the Staff Regiment, connected by phone with Cape Foca and the Cape Punta Sabbia at Lambi, informed Colonel Leggio that Linopoti's stronghold had fallen.

At 0700, Colonel Kenyon and Captain Saxton arrived at Ambavri Tactical Command. They brought no good information: no British reinforcements would arrive that day or in the next due to lack of naval vessels according to news received from the command in Cairo. Colonel Kenyon, therefore, asked Colonel Leggio to fire artillery at the landing areas and to destroy or, at least, damage enemy naval boats to reduce their reinforcements. Meantime it was also asked to maintain the actual positions. Colonel Leggio literally responded: "Be assured. The 10th will not give up one step".

Towards 0720 a soldier of Lieutenant Lorusso's platoon escaping from Mount Eremita reported that his officer had been captured with all his men.

Throughout the day, dozens and dozens of airplanes hammered the battlefield with bombs and machine guns. They dominated the battlefield.

At 1000 the anti-aircraft guns in the Cos area (about forty) ceased firing because they had been partly or completely destroyed by the enemy attacks.

Three German planes were shot down.

No Italian or English aircraft were noted flying during the battle on October 3 and 4. Only one duel was registered in Linopoti's sky,

In the afternoon, the 75/27 Artillery Battery at Ghermé was captured by the Germans who, afterwards, used the same artillery to shoot at the port of Cos and on the sea to hit boats with civilian and military men escaping capture and to destroy the remaining Italian defence settlements.

In the evening, the watch station at Cape Foca was burning.

At about 2030, Italian soldiers reported British men were escaping from the island floating on boards of any kind heading to the Turkish coast carrying equipment to save.

Sergeant major Rosso was sent to the British Command. On his return he confirmed the departure of the British. There was none, either officer or soldier in the city and at their offices.

By midnight the Italian situation worsened: the enemy had occupied the Italian Ammunition Depot near Ambavri and was about to occupy the houses on the town's outskirt. It was decided to retreat. The companies, almost decimated, took positions near the ancient Roman Theatre. The 5th Company was tasked to hinder the enemy advance because it had the task of supporting rear units during the day.

Since the Roman Theatre area was unsuitable to support a new enemy attack, Colonel Leggio and Lieutenant Colonel Bonserio Francesco, commanding officer of the 2nd Battalion, decided a second retreat at the first light of the day in the Saint Nicholas area towards Punta Forbici.

At the head of his platoon, Lieutenant Ballardino, 6th Company, was killed.

Lieutenant Vietri was seriously injured while he was at his gun of the Cannons Company; he died a few days later at the Hippocrates Hospital.

Captain Orlando Carlo had been hurt on his arm.

Liuetenant Piazza Giovanni, commanding officer 6th Company, was hit in his head. The bullet perforated his helmet. He was the one that by his enthusiasm, courage and expertise, had resisted, almost alone, the German attacks.

Lastly, many other soldiers died having fought for the Regiment and their Flag.

The 7th company with its commander, Lieutenant Massa, managed to retreat and take position in the Catholic cemetery.

Regiment Headquarters with its commanding officer, Captain Scotti, remained at Ambavri but in the morning of 4th was completely disbanded by heavy airstrike and by the German infantrymen reinforced during the night.

Cos town was occupied at 0700 on October 4.

As a liaison officer between the Regiment Command and the Units, at 0900 on day 4, I explained to Colonel Leggio the new situation in Saint Nicholas area. The enemy was advancing with small tanks armed with mortars. The defence settings from Cos to Punta Forbice (Lambi) was overwhelmed.

Colonel Leggio, Lieutenant Colonel Bonserio, Captains Colussi, Olivieri and myself as well as Lieutenant Citro, in view of the tragic situation (units disrupted and surrounded, due to the absolute supremacy of the Luftwaffe) decided to surrender. There was no more space to retreat and organize a defensive position with what had remained of the Regiment. At the back of our shoulders there was only the sea.

Captains Olivieri and Lieutenant Citro were sent as deputies for surrender.

Whilst I was informing Colonel Leggio on the departure of the two officers I was struck by a mortar splinter.

Shortly afterwards, the resistance in Cos ceased but before being captured, Colonel Leggio exalted his men having accomplished their duty and that they were forced to surrender due to enemy air supremacy.

Cos Sector - The Durham Light Infantry (DLI) Activities

Major David Rissik was an Aide Officer in the DLI. In 1952 he wrote the 1939 to '45 Durham Light Infantry's history. The relating part to the activities carried out by the Unit at Cos is reported in Chapter 7, p. 209 - 218. The story is based on the information gathered consulting all the officers and soldiers who survived the war on the island.

Below is an excerpt on the actions taken.

In the early hours of September 16, company C and Colonel Kirby were on board an aircraft when they learned their destination would be the island of Cos in the Dodecanese.

On the island there were about 3,000 Italians and the only landing base available in the archipelago except those of Rhodes. The DLI would have to take possession of Cos' airport in view of subsequent operations against Rhodes.

It was known that some German technicians were on the island and, in view of the capitulation of their Country, the Italians were now determined to remain inactive.

It was a lovely day when the first plane landed on Cos airport. With great surprise the new arrivals noticed the presence of a South African Spitfire squadron that arrived just before them, along with a parachutist company.

It took two days for most of the battalion to arrive at the destination, and the German air force was already beginning to be noticed: the fighters machine-gunned any mobile target and the bombers dumped their loads on the landing field and on the roads.

It had become urgent to fill the craters caused by the bombs in order to restore what was hit and to allow roads and air traffic to continue being used. Company C had the order to move to Cos town to assist in the ship unloading of materiel much needed on the island.

The A company of the battalion was the last to arrive on a landing strip quite damaged and spotted with flaming and steaming aircraft. The company missed one of its platoons flying in a Dakota aircraft that fell into the sea due to engine fault. The surviving occupiers were picked up by a Turkish kayak. Despite the immediate intervention of a British ship, they were not released. Perhaps the Turks wanted some money in exchange. The platoon spent some time in Turkey and in an internee camp. Company "A" had to do without it.

After the first 48 hours, all rifle companies (A, B, D) except the C were located around the airport but the Headquarter Company (HQ Coy) who had not arrived yet, nor the vehicles meant to arrive by ships.

The Italians did not show themselves particularly hostile but they did not cooperate in any way. On the other hand, German aircraft very active, made the troop operations on the ground quite difficult. It was attempted to transfer the Hurricanes and the Spitfires to an alternative strip in pressed soil at the outskirts of Cos and in the Salt Plain three miles away

Meantime two aircraft squadrons landed but they were immediately attacked. The Beaufighters intervened although they could not stay in action for a long time because of the fuel supply; their base was too far away and they could not compete with the manoeuvrable Messerschmidts.

The battalion was organically complete at the end of September.

Many of the German planes arrived from Russia were Junkers 88, painted white. The landing field at Antimachia was daily attacked and the damage, both human and material, increased more and more.

It was useless to make repairs because there were no British planes. The situation did not seem to change.

The A and B companies were ordered to move eastward to Cos town whilst company D, Commanding officer captain John Thorpe, was tasked to defend Antimachia airport to the fullest extent possible.

Companies A and B took position in an olive grove area five miles west of the harbour. Their task: give protection to allow the setting up of another landing ground near the salt lake.

On the night of October 3 the German air activity become intense. There was a suspect that saboteurs were parachuted.

At dawn the silence was broken by the intense noise of aircraft engines; the machineguns crackled along the northwest coast and a 75mm Italian artillery battery came into action.

The communication line between the battalion and company D on the airfield had been cut off; the German paratroopers landed in Antimachia but the news was only known after a long delay.

Colonel Kirby was in the hospital and Hugh Vaux, who replaced him, ordered the battalion to take the lead on the main road Cos - Antimachia. The enemy was now in sight as he was disembarking; meanwhile, company C, deployed along the periphery of the city, received the order to send a platoon to the south side of the island to ascertain where the enemy had landed. The platoon was devoid of transport because they had not yet come to the island and it was necessary to use a jeep. While performing the job, the patrol came into contact with the advance guard elements along the road Cos - Antimachia. Lieutenant Silverwight and his driver were killed.

The battle for the island had begun.

Colonel Kirby, as soon as he knew the situation, by a motorcycle reached the battalion. In the available short time, before the mass of the Germans could arrive in the vicinity, attempts were made to improve positions. It was not easy because the terrain was compact and rocky. Besides, there were only a handful of tools available.

Soon the Stuka appeared, bombing everywhere. Anti aircraft weapons were few and far apart. They circled in the air in search of possible targets to hit. British planes were completely absent.

The German infantry advanced and the fighting started seriously. Throughout the day the battalion was the object of the enemy attack.

The mortars of company B, north of the road, intervened with bomb launches achieving effective results.

The Germans attacked frontally but their action was also aimed at striking the sides of the deployment. Despite obstinate resistance, the company's B platoons were overwhelmed and lost contact with A company on its left, south of the road.

The prolonged resistance of British units is also due to Sergeant Major Flanagan's efforts to maintain constantly the ammunition supply and Major John Bush, the chief of supplies, which, despite intense fire and mortar bombs striking his warehouses, managed to support the units with food.

German pressure increased. For the battalion it was only a matter of time before being completely overwhelmed by the enemy's numerical disparity of men and equipment. Colonel Kirby ordered the antitank platoon at Lambi to stand on the right side of the HQ Coy. It served a little.

At 1700, the defending Cos town's company, the C, received the order to retire to the suburbs of the town. Company A had to stay south of the main route even if it had no contact with the rest of the battalion. During the swinging nature of the battle heavy losses were imposed on the Germans; even the battalion had suffered a lot and its composition was now less than 200 personnel. Captain Gray's A company had few men remaining and retreated to the west in the direction of the area of a 75mm Italian artillery battery still in action although heavily attacked by enemy planes.

The Italians were pressed not only by the air but also by an infantry attack from the east and west sprawled by the Germans who had landed in the southeastern part of the island.

Gray offered his contribution and stayed alongside the Italians until the evening when the enemy stopped to eat the evening meal, accompanying it with songs. It was then that Gray picked up his men and got ready to attack with the bayonet when a gunner appeared with the news that the rest of the battalion had gathered at Cos. Gray then decided to reach the other British units.

The remains of companies B and C had been deployed to form a defence perimeter on the west side of the town. The fight continued until late in the evening.

The enemy mortars action was more and more intense. The battalion commander ordered his men to shelter between the houses. John Bush was hit and died a bit later. He did the utmost in supplying the battalion all day long. Even Major Mark Leather and Captain Jack Stafford were hit. The situation was really critical. The battalion vice commander, Hugh Vaux, then got in touch with the superior command to be told what to do.

Supplies wouldn't arrive. The numerical disparity with the enemy was too big. He then gave the order to suspend any activity of contrast and divide all the remaining personnel into small groups, about a dozen, and reach the small village of Kargeon [13] up the hills, between Cos and Antimachia, about three miles to West from their present position. The men would have to carry their weapons and engage the enemy if necessary adopting guerrilla fighting. A mortar platoon was left behind to cover the evacuation until 0200 on the following morning. Each man received two bandoliers with ammunition, food and two blankets.

The transfer was not easy. It had to be done by tired soldiers at night time in rough terrain. There were clashes along the path with German patrols on the hills and the losses were heavy.

However, groups, gradually departed, began to arrive near Kargeon where they found shelter. Sixty men were counted, but, passing time, others came.

There was no food and hope was to get in the Italian food store but it was already occupied by the Germans.

A group of soldiers was detached to the beach and attempted to build a raft with which to reach Turkey, pick up a caique to fetch from the island the remaining men. When they arrived at the beach, near a cave, they found an

---

[13] The correct name of the village is KONIARGION between Pili (or Pellis as written by the British) and Asfendiu. There is another place "Stazzo/Sheepfold Kastoglou" located near the Terme, SE of the island. The owners, Kastoglou family, originally sheep farmers, reports that many British fugitives were housed and refreshed by them in October 1943.

English captain of the Special Boat Service [14] who informed them of the next arrival of a caique at two o'clock in the night for the withdrawal of the British. So it happened. All those who had gathered in the village, eight officers and just over 60 men, managed to find a place on the boat and head to Turkey.

It was October 13, the time spent hiding was 9 days during which all suffered from hunger. They had to thank Greek farmers who brought them food.

During the sailing, next to the Turkish coast, the personnel onboard were ordered to throw into the water all the available weapons. It was necessary since they should be considered shipwreck survivors. Once in Turkey, with another boat made available by the British Service, the troops reached Kastellorizo and hence finally Egypt.

Antimachia Sector - Italian activity

(Aiello) [15] In those days and until they landed, the Germans carried out a number of bombing and machine-gun operations on the airport. Numerous British fighters were hit while trying to counter German incursions. Only two German airplanes were shot down by the British/Italian island's defence: one was hit by Lieutenant Morganti flying the last remaining efficient Italian fighter; a second one was shot down by the Italian antiaircraft 75/27 A.V. battery.

Orders and directives transmitted by the island's command excluded the possibility of a German landing from the sea and admitted only the hypothesis of sabotage actions by parachutist troops. That was explained and repeatedly explained in many ways and said, again and again, inculcated in every officer and soldier's mind on the island.

On October 3, the German landing at Cos took place.

---

[14] It is a UK Navy Service and along with Air Force Service, Reconnaissance and Special Forces Group constitute the U.K. Special Forces under a Directorate.
[14] Antony Rogers, *Churchill's folly, Leros and the Aegean. The Last Great British Defeat of World War Two*, Cassel Military Paperbacks, U.K., capitol 4, pag. 56
[15] Artillery Observer

During the night there was a strong movement of British air convoys and in the morning some ships were expected to arrive. That is why it was not possible to distinguish the nationality of the approaching vessels; the noises heard were considered to be caused by British ships.

The company of Captain Kuhlmann landed in the area of Silogremmo - Kamari Bay, South West of the island. I saw the approaching boats before entering the fire batteries range of the 62nd, 63rd, 64th, 246th and the 136th. They, although immediately warned by myself, hesitated to open fire waiting for superior orders. The batteries fire began when the German assault boats had already come to the beach.

At the same time, a hundred paratroopers came down from six Junkers at a very low altitude. They landed on the isthmus cutting immediately any communication between the units placed on the East side of the isthmus and the ones on the West towards Kefalo : my observatory, a company of machine guns (12th) reinforced by a coastal platoon, two anti-tank sections, a flame section and an 81mm mortar section.

Considering my task as observer was over, I put my artillerymen and myself at the disposal of the company commander, Lieutenant De Giovanni.

Meanwhile, paratroopers (on the isthmus) and landing troops (from Kamari Bay) had already seized the 136th battery although they offered heavy resistance. On it the 246th opened suppressive fire immediately, so did the 12th company mortars and the anti-cannon guns of which I had taken command.

The Germans, having left groups of soldiers to face our company, headed for the centre of the island. Shortly thereafter, the 246th was also taken.

It has to be noticed that due to the positions of two batteries {136th and 246th} it was impossible to organize a close defence. They tried to stop the Germans by firing at zero-point pallet grenades.

The 1st Battalion, positioned in Kardamena area, was hastily and incompletely gathered and sent towards the enemy under incessant aerial attacks, weakly thwarted by our antiaircraft batteries.

The British 40 mm gun crews, like all other English troops, had already fled. The British on the island (almost two thousand) were dispersed in the fields or awaiting to be taken prisoners in caverns and wolloons. Most of them, those who were able to, abandoned weapons and materials, went to Cos along the fields to try to embark on the boats heading to the coast of Turkey.

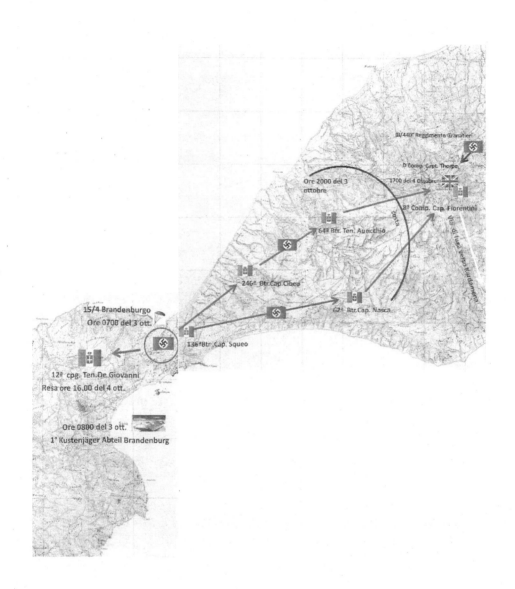

West Sector covering Antimachia and Kamari Bay

72

It also happened that the British fired from the harbour with machine guns and 40 mm cannons against boats loaded with Italian soldiers and local people fleeing to Turkey whilst they were deserting the fighting.

The battalion commander, Lieutenant Colonel Castrogiovanni, not knowing the speedy advance of the Germans, drove the battalion toward the 246th battery. He marched even before the platoon explorer. He was captured by paratroopers. At the first contacts with the German troops, the battalion broke away and all the soldiers wandered disorderly across the valleys to reach Antimachia area. The 62nd battery, under the command of Captain Camillo Nasca, immediately raised a German flag and joined the enemy. The Germans stopped along the Placa stream, placing their command on the 62nd battery at Cristalochia.

In the early afternoon they began to advance towards Antimachia airport. The 62nd battery received the order to open fire against the Italian-British airfield's positions. The gun crews refused to do so, the battery commander and his subordinate, Lieutenant Piero Pierraymond, fired three gun shots against English emplacements. This was the only action the battery did in favour of the Germans.

Captain De Flaviis had taken command of the battalion remains being the senior officer. He consulted with Major Paola, deputy commander of the antiaircraft artillery, and, examined how useless might be resistance action, at 1600 he ordered the surrender to the enemy.

Lieutenant Auricchio, commander of the 64th battery, wanted to try an extreme resistance action having gathered and organized a large number of fugitive infantrymen. The Germans sent to him some other Italian officers to convince him to desist from any resistance action and he was persuaded.

Meanwhile, the 12th company received encouragement support and promises of solicitous reinforcements both by Admiral Mascherpa from Lero and by the British Command of Cyprus through the Navy radio station up at Mount Timianò. At first the arrival of a battalion from Lero by 1600 was anticipated; then British reinforcements would have arrived in the evening. Subsequently, the reinforcements were postponed on the night and, at dawn the following day. Cyprus even specified as "formidable" the announced reinforcements.

The waiting was exhausting. Time was passing by without seeing any friends arrive. No reinforcement at all to justify the hard resistance. The island was completely German hunting ground. An exception was due to an Italian seaplane from Lero's base; it came in the early hours of day 3, flew above us to carry out a torpedo action against German ships. The pilot was attacked by three German fighters. He tried to juggle and defend himself. Having understood the impossibility to dare any more, perhaps struck, directed the plane against a German destroyer. The ship exploded and sunk.

On the ground, at the end of the evening, the fire among the opposite factions slowed down until it ceased. At 0600, October 4, other paratroopers came down from Junkers just ahead of our lines. Our machine guns immediately fired against the descending paratroopers and many were killed before touching the ground. A few hours later the Germans attacked our line in strength and once again they were repelled.

In the early hours of the afternoon, the Germans attacked supported by tanks with twin guns. It was preceded by a fierce fire of 88mm guns accompanied and supported by their aviation with machine gunning and bombing. Lieutenant De Giovanni, considering it useless to resist on the line of the isthmus, gave orders to retreat on Mount Timianò. It was impossible: the troops were engaged in close contact with the enemy and those who managed to get out were rounded up by the German mechanized vehicles.

Lieutenant De Giovanni and a very small number of soldiers, reached Mount Timianò which was subject to heavy Stuka's bombing. Then he surrendered to a German outpost, who had already surrounded the position. From that moment, on October 4, the battle had ceased on the island.

Antimachia Sector - "D" Company Activities

A report drawn up by an unknown D company officer stored in the DLI Museum at Durham - Durham County – England - describes minutely the events from the 3 to 23 October 1943.

The war events are reported only on day 3; in the following days he wrote on how they escape the capture of the unit along the valleys and up to the neighbouring hills of Antimachia, avoiding encounters and clashes with German soldiers. Only on October 22, after nineteen days hidden in the bushes whilst receiving food from the Greek peasants, the British managed to sail to Turkey.

3rd October, 1943 – Sunday

Island invaded at dawn by German paratroopers that were seen landing approximately six miles South of Landing Ground (Antimachias). Estimated numbers 100, seaborne were also used, some landing on the West and North coast. The Coy. Comdr. Capt. I.H.Thorpe on being informed of this, ordered 17Pl, under command of Sgt. Filis and 1Mortar (3^{in}) Detachment to proceed to Windmill Hill which is situated at the West end of the Landing Ground. The Coy. Comdr. then made out paratroops and despatched by D.R. (Pte Buglass). This D.R. did not return, whether he arrived at Bn.H.Q. we were unable to find out. Time of departure of D.R. approximately 0500. All lines of communication with Bn.H.Q. were useless by this time. The Signal N.C.O. L/Cpl Sillitoe failed to get in touch with Bn.H.Q. with 18 Set; all 38 Sets which each Platoon had were unable to contact Coy.H.Q.

Coy. Comdr. decided to move up to the Windmill Hill, time 0550, on arrival he placed Cpl. Bills' detachment of 3" Mortars in position. During this period Capt. White had taken over 17 Pl., and moved towards Ginger Hill which is situated on the South side of the Landing Ground. On Ginger Hill he would most likely join up with 18 Pl. that was under command of Lt. Ryves, and attached to this Platoon was Sgt. Wilsons's detachment of 3 Mortars.

Coy. Comdr. stayed on Windmill Hill until approximately 1645. At 1600 hrs. I went onto Windmill Hill and the situation there was that Coy. Comdr. was in charge of 16 Pl and he had also managed to hold on to an Italian Captain and approximately 60 men, but on receipt of a message from the Antimachia direction, the Italian Captain withdrew to the North side of the village. Message stated that the Germans were advancing on Antimachia from Pillis and Asfendiu. All day long 87's and 88's bombed L.G. and area forward of his own troops.

By 0900 hours it appeared to me as though there were only 2 Bofors Guns left in working condition.

At 1530 hours there was no more Ack Ack fired from the South end of the Island, from 0845 hours the Colonel of the 1ˢᵗ L.A.A. Regt. R.A. and his adjutant were at my Coy.H.Q. every now and then the Colonel went over to the Windmill Sector which was situated on the East side of Antimachia about 600'.

At 1700 hours all R.A. personnel, that is the Colonel, Adjutant, 1 Major, 1 Padre, M.O., C.S.M. Price, and a couple of gunners moved off to a Wadi about 100 yds to the East of Sector, this was the last time that this party was seen by me.

At 1730 the Coy. Comdr.gave the order to destroy all documents this was done by fire, Coy.H.Q. then moved back to an area about 300 yds to the North (position of the Coy.H.Q. was approximately 400 yds. West of the fork roads North of Antimachia). The Coy. Comdr. then ordered the CSM and the remainder of Coy.H.Q. to wait in the Wadi, while he observed the German advance from the North.

At 1750 five 87's came over, they were diving to drop their bombs when the forward troops of Jerry put up a Very light (white) so they banked and dropped the bombs, seven in all, a distance of six yards from us. The Coy. Comdr. was wounded in the small of the back left side. The shrapnel passed through his web belt cutting the left buckle; wound did not bleed very much, put on a field dressing. This was last raid of the day. Coy. Comdr, Pte Proudlock and myself then moved over to pick up the remainder of Coy.HQ but we were unable to do so, these men were not seen any more. The Germans that took Windmill were estimated by the Coy. Comdr. to have come up the Wadi due West from the sea. We now moved on from this position to approximately halfway to Cardamena, which is situated on the east Coast, travelling by jeep down the main road. Halted by Italian Road Block, we wanted to stay with them for the night but they made us move on. So travelled a little more and pulled up at a building where we slept for the night.

4th October, 1945 – Monday

Moved off at dawn by Jeep towards Cardamena, pulled off the road at approximately 400' from the town, after putting Jeep out of action, we moved into a Wadi. Stayed here for about one hour, when we observed movement on our left under a small group of trees. On a closer inspection found them to be British Troops, so we decided to move over to join them. The party consisted of four officers, R.A. and about 35 O.R's – whether the O.R's were all RA I cannot state. During the period from 0100 to 1150 hours 87's came over in batches of fives and dive-bombed the town of Cardamena and the area to our North and West. During the bombing the Germans did not appear to be advancing from his position of the previous night. We decided to move from present position to the foot of hills North of Cardamena. At 1200 we moved, after travelling about 100' we took cover behind a wall with a couple of trees to shade us from the air, and another raid of 87's with fighter escort. Again moved on but had to lie flat owing to the fighters and one Dornier seaplane coming at a height of 200'.

Again moved on toward small village at the foot of the hills, but this was not our luck, time now 1730 approximately. This time we saw 2 German lorries with trailers and a Mortar on each with roughly 20 men on each coming from Pillis or Asfendiu. They passed us by about 4 yards, all troops seemed to be well armed, so we lay still until the moon came up. Whilst lying down I heard the Germans attacking Cardamena, their lorries did not come back along the same road. At 2015 we moved on to a small village, where we slept under the trees for the night.

5th October, 1943 – Tuesday

After breakfast and dressing of Coy. Comdr's wound, which appeared to be no better, if anything it was swelling. He felt very stiff in the back when we had to move. We stayed in position till 1345, when a Greek warned us to move as the Germans were coming to search the area. During the morning a Greek woman brought a matchbox to us. On reading message inside this is how it ran "Who are you? I am Pte. Walters of the S.A.S. Regt." His number was included, but the chitty was lost. I replied by merely stating Three English soldiers. After warning we moved up into small waste area and stayed till dark, then again moved into the hills for the night.

6th October, 1943 – Wednesday.

We are now in position on hillside overlooking Pellis and the North of the island. During day observed Dornier seaplanes moving in pairs at irregular intervals. These planes travelling from dawn till dusk, patrolling the waters, they appeared to me to travel to Rhodes and back again. 87's were going over in batches of 9's to what I believed to be Leros. At dark moved over towards Asfendiu and higher into hills. Pte. Proudlock very dizzy and shivering – suspected sandfly bite.

7th October, 1943 – Thursday.

This was a very good position for observation of North Coast. Saw 3 German landing craft, later learnt from Navy that they were called "F. Boats" These craft pulled in and unloaded on West side of Salt Flats about 700' along coast. Transport left the area of the Hospital and returned by circular routes. Wound of Coy. Comdr. no better. 2 Greeks fed us for a day and stayed the night owing to the Pte being in a worse condition. 87's and 88's were over us for 8th.

8th October, 1943- Friday.

Same position and fed by Greeks. German seaplanes same as for the 6th. 87's and 88's as for previous day. At 1715 watched a small convoy of 3 ships (Merchant). These were joined by the 3 F. Boats from the North Coast and a further 2 that appeared to come from the town of Cos.

They all moved over to the island about 3 miles from Cos rough bearing of N.N.W. Coy. Comdr. and Pte still in same condition – stayed night.

9th October 1943 – Saturday.

Still in same position. Normal air activity by Germans. Coy. Comdr. and Pte same condition. Coy. Comdr's wound turning black on top side, now at the end of F. Dressing.

10th October, 1943 – Sunday.

Officer decided owing the condition of wound and the condition of Pte Proudlock to go into hospital (German occupied), the following day. At 1800 hours I moved off with them to a shepherd's house at the foot of a hill, on arrival at the house the Greeks gave bread and cheese, so after burning the Company's A.F.R. 122's I left the Capt. and Pte. Proudlock with the best of health. Air activity normal. 5 F Boats returned from the island N.N.W. of Cos, 3 to position on North coast and 2 moved to the harbour of Cos, my estimation. I then moved off in a Southerly direction toward Cardamena not known whether officer and Pte. went into hospital –never saw them.

11th October, 1943 – Monday.

Arrival on hilltop overlooking Cardamena and Antimachia at 0330 and slept till 0900. Observed all day, nothing of importance except there appeared to be movement on the L.G. at Antimachia, i.e. 8 lorries moving up and down the strip. The two Macchi planes (Fighter) which the British moved from one of the pens and put to one side away from the strip appeared to have been taken on to L.G. which I took for the purpose of decoy. At night moved to bottom of hills and slept till daylight.

12th October, 1943 – Tuesday

Today received the news from a Greek that 12 English soldiers were in a house on hillside, so I packed up and joined this party. Strengh of party including myself 15.

Names and unit as follows: Sgt. Burridge (M.M.) R.A. - F/Sgt. Taylor, R.A.F. – Sgt. Phillipotts, R.A.F. (Cypher Branch) – L/Bdr. Thompson, R.A. – Gnr. Webb, R.A. – LAC Moreton - LAC. Prince - LAC. Terry – LAC. Nichols – LAC. Gargon – LAC. Edwards – LAC. Luke – LAC. Scott – LAC Riley.

Pte Walters of the S.A.S.Regt. had left his kit in a Wadi but nothing was seen of the man himself. 2 Officers R.A.F., F/Lt. R.G. Allan and Lt. Highland lived in a cave above the white house, but refused to take over the party or even their own men.

13th October, 1943 – Wednesday

Living in a house. Rained all day. No Greek visitors. 3 Ju 88's appeared to take off from North end of Island, nothing else happened.

14th October, 1943 – Thursday

Still in the house. Fine weather. Note written in French received at 1900 hours to the effect that we were to follow the Guide. Here 2 Italian soldiers joined party. After journey of approximately 6½ miles over mountains, and keeping close to the shore, arrived safely at destination and contacted Greek with letter signed by Naval Comdr. appeared O.K. Boat did not answer signals by Greek Agent.

15th October, 1943 – Friday

Stayed on in a cave all day with Greek Agent. Expected boat at night so the Agent and myself sent up Signal Flashes from the beach from 2100 till 0230 hours – nothing arrived.

16th October, 1943 – Saturday

Same procedure as for 15th

17th October, 1943 – Sunday

Agent decided to go to Turkey in small boat to bring back launch. 2 more Italians joined party. No small boat available this day.

18th October, 1943 – Monday

Agent went out to get a boat himself, but ran into a German patrol of 12 strong. These men wore white caps. Agent returned, we made raft, but it was of no use.

19th October, 1943 – Tuesday

Made another raft under supervision of the Agent, but when tried out this also failed. At 1930 hours the R.A.F. Officers returned to join party but when they saw the party was still as large, they moved off to a water point about 1½ miles away.

20th October, 1943 – Wednesday

Made another raft for the Agent. Raft excellent in water so Agent moved off at 1930 hours. Appeared to be making good progress on a calm sea.

21th October, 1943 – Thursday

Greeks arrived and told us that the Germans were now living on the hillside. They had evacuated Cardamena, Antimachia, so now we were on one side of hill and Germans on another. At 1100 lours approximately sent message to the 2 R.A.F. Officers to move to cave at dark as boat was expected tonight.

22th October, 1943 – Friday

At 0150 boat arrived. All were on board by 0220 hours. Once on all arms were handed over to the Skipper of the boat under orders from F/Lt. R.G. Allan who had now taken over. The following arms and ammunition were handed over: 3 T.M.C., 2 Rifles, 2 Pistols Revolver .45., 166 Rds. .45., 122 .303 Ball, 9 Steel Helmets and a few pieces of equipment.

Landed on a small Island off the Turkish mainland, picked up again at 1530. Prior to being picked up, Sgt. Phillpotts, R.A.F., Cypher Dep. was sent to the mainland by small sailing boat. He was admitted Hospital. We were taken to the mainland where after waiting for the Officers being questioned, etc. we moved over to the other side of Harbour and boarded L.C.T's 139 and 114.

23th October, 1943 – Saturday

Moved off at 1900 approximately on board a 2 masted fishing boat. On board 17 British Troops, including R.A.F. and 33 survivors of the HMS Hurworth (Destroyer). The Greek Adrius and Hurworth were both sunk by mines on the Friday night at 2300.

Journey to Castel Rosso was uneventful, arrived safely at 1030 a.m. on 27th. F/Lt. R.G. Allan and Lt Highland with 7 R.A.F. Regt. left the same night on board R.A.F. Launch.

My party of seven in all left at midnight and 28th arriving Haifa – no enemy seen during voyage.

Appendix "A"

List of Officers and other Rank casualties as known when last seen by me or by other personnel evacuated with me.

- Lt.Col. R.F. KIRBY Comd.1st Bn D.L.I.
  Shrapnel wound left side face and left knee. Left in Cos temporary Hospital
  PW. 3.10.43
- Major K.M. LEATHER, OC. HQ Coy, 1st Bn. D.L.I.
  Shrapnel wound upper left arm and shoulder, considerable loss of blood. Left in Cos. Temporary Hospital
  PW. 3.10.43
- Capt. S. STAFFORD . OC B Coy 1st Bn. D.L.I.
  Shrapnel wound right thigh. Left in Cos temporary Hospital
  PW. 3.10.43

- Capt. & QM F. Bush, M.B.E. 1st Bn. D.L.I.
  Died of wounds   3.10.43
- Capt. S.SILVERWIGHT OC Carrier Plt. 1st Bn. D.L.I.
  Last seen in Bantam which was hit by MG fire while on move and
  somersaulted off road   3.10.43
- Lieut. HABGOOD, Pl. Comdr."B" Coy 1st Bn. D.L.I.
  Last seen in forward position which was being subjected to intense antytank
  gun fire and mortar bombing. No further movement seen and position
  overrun by enemy. Thought killed.   3.10.43
- C.S.M. MOODY, HQ Coy 1st Bn. D.L.I.
  Killed - shot through heart   3.10.43
- Lieut. F. HUDGON, Pl. Comdr."B" Coy 1st Bn. D.L.I.
  Last seen when in hand to hand fighting with enemy.
  Thought killed.   3.10.43
- Capt. R. SIMMONS, 21/c A tk Pl. 1st Bn. D.L.I.
  Last seen with Pl covering withdrawal to hills.   4.10.43
- Lieut. NEWCOMBE, Pl. Comdr."C" Coy 1st Bn. D.L.I.
  Known to have surrendered   P.W. 4.10.43
- Lieut. R. SMITH, Pl. Comdr."C" Coy 1st Bn. D.L.I.
  Last seen with party covering withdrawal to hills.   4.10.43
- Lieut. ROBINSON, Pl. Comdr. 1st Bn. D.L.I.
  Known to have surrendered   P.W. 4.10.43
- Capt. ELLIS, Intelligence Officer 1st Bn. D.L.I.
  Last seen in hills.   4.10.43

The following personnel, were all with "D" Coy. , 1st Bn. D.L.I.,
2 dets Mortar Pln., 1 Sec. Carrier last heard of defending
Antimachia L.G. 3.10 43 .

Capt. J. THORPE   OC "D" Coy
Capt. M. WAIT   2 i/c "D" Coy
Lieut. REVES   The Buffs Regt. Pl Comdr D Coy
Capt. MacDONALD   RAMC, Unit MO
          Left in Cos Temporary Hospital with wounds   PW 3.10.43
Rev. WRIGHT, Ch.F.   Unit Padre
          Left in Cos Temporary Hospital with wounds   PW 3.10.43

COMMUNICATION MARASMA

To have an idea of the confusion which reigned in those early hours of the morning of October 3, it is enough to read the words of Sergeant Esposito Giuseppe's report in which, having introduced himself with these words: *telegraphic engineer; decorated with two War Crosses; honoured by a solemn Dodecanese Governor encomium; enrolled in 1935, February the 1st and sent to Cos island in 1939, August 22nd; returned from captivity in a Macedonia prisoner camp,* declares:

(Esposito) *On October 2, 1943, while on duty at Prophet Elia stronghold switchboard, along with private Abate Gino, communication activities were more intense than usual. At 2330 I was told by the 10th Infantry Regiment Command to pass on the information of the arrival of a tanker from Leros the following morning, at 0530. Immediately the message was transferred to the telephone operators on the island.*

On 3 October at 0040 an air alarm, previously reported by Leros, was launched. At 0250 "the ceased alarm" was given.

Ten minutes later, at 0300, I was signaled by the Marmari watch station that five ships, some of which were quite big, had appeared between Calimno and Pserimo islands. Immediately I hurried to pass on the information to the Signal Centre using PAPA system.

The officer on duty, Captain Floccia, answered me with a trivial phrase (do not break me ...) On the contrary he asked me "Are you aware of the phonogram about the arrival of the tanker from Leros?"

I answered back somewhat angrily and I pointed out to him it was early for the tanker to arrive, instead in that precise moment I was talking about ships between the two islands in front of Cos. Captain Floccia ordered me to take strictly care of my duty.

Meanwhile, Marmari and Tingaki watch stations did not leave me a moment of respite by pointing out further movements of the sighted vessels and asking for orders in that regard.

For the second time I urgently called Captain Floccia, but he did not reply. I then phoned the stronghold commander, Lieutenant Coratza Salvatore who, after advising me to keep calm, got in touch both with the named captain and Colonel Leggio. The latter said not to worry, nothing would have happened. However, he said, be ready but don't open fire.

Later, I learned from the colonel's mistress he had been with her on the night from 2 to 3, and the one who answered on the phone had been his aide, Captain Colussi. Partly assured, I immediately took up an accurate watch and defence service of the line and the telephone exchange.

The Regiment Staff Officer got in touch with his British opposite number to find out if any of their convoy was due to arrive. The answer was negative.

The two stations at Marmari and Tingaki, the regimental platoons, the English hospital and the Royal Carabinieri no longer responded to my calls. It meant that they had been captured by the Germans.

At 0500, finally, the naval alert was launched, but it was too late for the enemy had already landed. In any case, I conveyed the received order. I was informed that reinforcement measures had been taken to help Linopoti stronghold. They never arrived. The Commanders of the 2nd 81 mm mortars company, the 8th machine gun company and anti-paratrooper platoon, ordered their men to retreat on Mount Dikeus.

The Luftwaffe planes dropped bombs and machine-gunned all over the area. Hundreds of German paratroopers dropped in various spots.

Our artillery remained silent; only the antiaircraft guns were shooting desperately. In one of the last phone calls, Captain Olivieri, from the Staff Office, asked for news. I told him all communications were interrupted and I expressed my disappointed with the deplorable attitude of the Regiment Command. Captain Olivieri replied with encouragement and patriotic words. While talking to the captain, the Germans came in. I took off my headset and violently broke it on the table. Then I was taken out, disarmed and stripped of everything.

CONSIDERATION OF THE BATTLE

Lieutenant Zucchelli was the Italian officer in command of the Italian Royal Carabinieri. After the German assault to the island he was allowed to maintain his command so as order could be preserved among the population.

At the end of the war, before his repatriation, in Rhodes, he handed a report to the Italian Affairs Committee covering the period 1943 – 1945. The following is his crude report [16]: *One of the factors that severely overwhelmed the defensive action of the Italian garrison is to be found in the lack of the Nation's homogeneity, consciences and military efficiencies that emerged after September the 8th. It may even be said that such separation began from July 25th when, with a questionable criterion, the "Black Shirts" (Fascists) were left in their posts in the defence system as it was believed by some Commanding Officers that it would have been sufficient for a slight modification to their uniforms and ask for their word of honour of loyalty to change their minds.*

Another reason must be sought in the moral and psychological situation in which the soldiers of the Aegean garrisons found themselves after the armistice. The troops were materially unprepared to support the conflict because, for the great majority, they were men for too long kept in military indolence but, inadvertently, called into action; morally because they were too impregnated with an absurd propaganda that had kept them in the dark of the real situation. There was also the seriousness of facing an enemy who until yesterday was a friend; an enemy lazily considered as such, while, for his part, was determined to be it. It took time because the ideas and feelings of disagreement, which had come into being within the "cadres", would have been settled. Unfortunately, time was not enough and at the time of the conflict there were still too many unit commanders caught by indecision and others, few fortunately, still deciding to keep faith to old fascist propaganda.

---

[16] Comando Generale Arma dei Carabinieri, Archivio Storico

An example: Captain Johnson, dropped in by parachute on the night of 10 to 11 September, was kept aloof awaiting the Italian military chief's decision. It was taken on the night of 12 when Johnson was asked to contact Cairo .

The arrival of the allies in Cos between 13 and 15 September contributed to the Italian crisis.

The Allied soldiers' behaviour, cold, reserved and, in some cases, hostile could only deeply irritate the well-known expansiveness of the Italians who had accepted with enthusiasm and generous affection the new friends. Moreover, the arrival of new troops and, especially, the wide promises created an exaggerated and definitely harmful sense of security in their minds.

The approach and the disembarkation of German troops on the island of Cos are the most amazing part for those familiar with the area and the defensive settlement, so as to appear incomprehensible. Admitting that enemy forces could approach the coast of the island in the area where it actually happened would have seemed crazy and unreasonable before it took place. Getting to land on Marmari, Masticari and Tingaki beaches, coming directly from Pserimo, it was absurd to think of it before then. The area, a bare beach, is the end of a vast plain of which even one square metre could not escape the artillery firing positioned on the whole island. Very few cannons and 81 mm mortars would have been enough to destroy the enemy whilst still deployed at sea, while a few heavy weapons would have been enough to prevent a single man from reaching the beach.

No cannon fired before the enemy had reached safe positions; no weapon intervened to prevent the advance of the attackers until they had achieved real superiority. Still, it couldn't be identified as a surprise since the alarm had been given throughout the island by the guards even when the attackers were away from the coast, defenceless on their little boats.

There were many civilians and soldiers from the highlands of the island witnessing the approach of the ships and boats to Tingaki – Marmari or Kardamena. Military telephones along the coastline were getting hot, the lines informing of approaching German landings when they were in their delicate and dangerous phase. Despite this, the Germans landed at Tingaki without receiving resistance except in Linopoti village on the main road Cos – Kefalo.

I had the opportunity, right after the disaster, to inquire on the peculiarity of such an event with some German officers able to know about the position they were in and for the part they had to play.

Someone said having passed Linopoti's dwelling, it was easy to cut in two halves the strength of the defence. Such an operation assumed decisive gravity because it added another negative factor undermining the moral and the spirit of the defenders.

Everyone argued that with the British at home it could no longer be considered possible for the Germans to attack. In the end, it was general knowledge that this meant not only the presence of a thousand Englishmen and Indians but of all the allied forces, with the Middle East Army not too distant. Creating such a mentality was contributed effectively by the English propaganda itself. There was no person on Cos who did not know that the allies' intention was to make the island an efficient air base for directing actions against Rhodes and Crete.

It was not difficult to admit so much. There was enough to notice the disproportion between the enormous quantity of material and supplies, the number of men, the feverish task of commands about the arrangement of the available equipment and the ones announced to be delivered, the efficient action in preparing a new airport in Torre di Lambi, in addition to the one already in existence in Antimachia and works for a third airfield. In short, as the days passed, the number of those who dared to take seriously the possibility of a German attack was diminishing greatly.

The Germans themselves must have considered absurd their chances. More than one of their officers then confessed that the attack on Cos was considered desperate but hopeless. For them it was necessary to maintain free the navigation routes into the Aegean in order to avoid the choking of the Rhodes and Crete units. Eventually some came to complain about the good result of their attack as it meant being forced to move on to Leros which was considered even more absurd. They themselves were the first to be surprised at the success of their action. The relative ease of the first step and the hardest, the landing, gave them hope that they did not have irresistible decisive fighters

Seeing an enemy opposite, even before it was known an enemy existed; looking at him appearing everywhere; feeling the sound of his weapons on

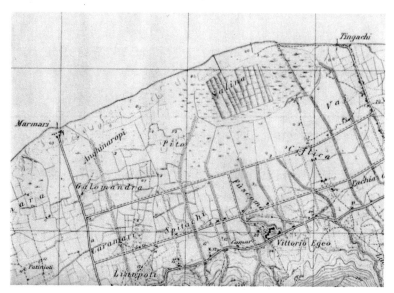

The Landing Area : Marmari – Tingachi
IGM – Asfendiu – Isola di Coo – Tav 25.000

View of the Landing Shore

The Landing Area, view from the sea

each side when there was still hope knowing he was busy getting off the landing boats, it could not seem a useful propaganda for a defender who, among other things, had never had the opportunity to hear whistling on his head of a diving plane. Nevertheless the units were forced to act on their own initiative, for lack of communications, each independent of the other.

This made it possible to believe in more than one unit that the others had ceased to fight, so to be the only one to face the entire enemy contingent. The unusual sight of enemy airplanes flying undisturbed in the sky, free to dive, to machine-gun and bomb, exacerbated the feeling of emptiness and isolation.

The defenders'morale was sustained by the hope of the immediate arrival of allied reinforcements. At least a plane to contrast the obsession of the Stuka so tremendously free to make their mortal play or, a ship appearing on the horizon.

People of all ages, sex, and religions dispersed everywhere in desperate search for a safe place, contributing with their screams of terror to spread distrust that was increasing in time.

Knowing how great confidence the British had shown in the outcome of the fighting it seemed unbelievable they were running to the beach to board any kind of available boats aiming for the Anatolian coast to escape from the battle: it was on the evening of October the 3rd.

The distant and near weapons ceased to fire. There was only the threatening blasts of the German mortar bombs launched on the harbour against the boats carrying escaping soldiers.

The depressing silence, however, seemed to be a sign of a struggle that would resume the following dawn with a favourable result. In the city, some were still confident in reinforcements coming. They did not. The silence of the weapons did not mean a truce but the end of all.

The Germans remained nested around the city. They did not trust to enter the town with the darkness of the night. What was considered an absurdity is it happened in less than 24 hours. Yet there was still on the island those who refused to surrender to the events and to the enemy: Lieutenant Francesco De Giovanni.

REPORTS ON THE BATTLE BY
THE MEDIA AND THE BRITISH GOVERNMENT

The Battle reported by the Media

Below are the texts of the media to communicate the war activities that took place on the island of Cos at the beginning of October 1943.

In Berlin on **October 4, 1943**, the Deutsch Nationalbibliothek- DNB reported the following:

Striking fights on the island of Cos

The island of Cos, northwest of Rhodes, in the Dodecanese, has recently been occupied by British troops. Badoglio's troops obviously contributed to the success of the action. The island was primarily an air base of the Royal Air Force since then. From that airport they led their attacks on the island of Rhodes.

Yesterday morning several landing groups reached the coast of Cos. They, using fast and landing boats, were able to reach the coast without being discovered. As a result of that decisive offensive, all the important targets of the island were captured in a short time. The enemy, surprised, could only defend a few points. There have been a great number of deaths.

More than 200 British soldiers were captured. The remaining military fled to the mountains in the centre of the island very difficult to control, abandoning, in addition to various material, four heavy bombing aircraft.

The TIMES in London on **5 October** reported:

GARRISON'S DESPERATE STRUGGLE

From our own correspondent – Cairo Oct. 4

The latest news from the Dodecanese island of Cos, although scanty, at least indicates that fighting is still going on, but the information revealed by the official report that the enemy "landed in strength" augurs a disparate struggle for our garrison. Strenuous attempts have been made ever since the island was taken to neutralize some of the many aerodromes around Cos, in Crete, Rhodes and Greece; but our own air bases are mostly far distant, and it has been an uphill struggle. The R.A.F. continued their task yesterday, and in addition to shooting down enemy aircraft over Cos, scored hits on shipping and airfields.

ENEMY CAPTURES SEVERAL IMPORTANT POINTS

The following joint Middle East war report was issued yesterday.

The enemy landed in strength on Cos on Sunday and secured several important points. Fighting continues.

Enemy shipping off the island of Cos was attacked from the air throughout Monday, many hits being scored. Beaufighters, Baltimores and Hudsons took part in these operations. Two Ju87s attempting to bomb the airfield were destroyed by our fighters and others were damaged.

GERMAN ACCOUNT OF THE RAID

The Berlin wireless said last night: The island of Cos, north-west of Rhodes, which was occupied some time ago by British formations, has served since as a base for British air forces from which Rhodes was also attacked. On Sunday morning all important military installation of the island were captured in a determined attack by several German landing groups, which approached the coast undiscovered with assault and landing boats.

The British, surprised resisted strongly at some points only and had a number of men killed. Over 200 British were captured uninjured. Some of the British soldiers fled into the inaccessible mountains in the interior of the island. Four British heavy bombers were among the aircraft captured. - British United Press

The TIMES in London **on 6 October** reported:

OPERATION IN THE DODECANESE
THE FIGHT FOR COS
RAPID GERMAN ACTION
From Our Military Correspondent

The report hitherto received about Cos has been brief and disjoined, but, pending a detailed official account a summary of these is useful. It is not known on what date Cos was captured by British Forces, but our Special Correspondent in Istanbul first reported its occupation on September 19. He stated that another island of the Dodecanese, Leros, had been occupied simultaneously and that we had gained also possession of Samos. This large island does not form part of the Dodecanese, but had been seized by the Germans after the campaign in Greece.

On September 21, two days later, our correspondent in Cairo, reported that an official announcement on the subject had been made and that the R.A.F. was using the airfield at Cos. On September 22 he stated that hostile aircraft had been attacking our positions and that so far 11 of them had been shot down.

Little more was heard about the island until October 3, when the German landing was officially announced. Our Cairo correspondent stated on that day that the island was lightly held and that, at all events for some days after our occupation had began, the antiaircraft artillery had been manned by Italians.

LANDING IN STRENGTH

On October 4 it was reported officially that the landings were in strength, that the enemy had secured important points and that his shipping off the island had been attacked from the air. The Germans for their part claimed that all important military installations had been taken together with 200 prisoners and that some of our troops had retired to the mountains.

It will be seen that, presuming the first report to have followed shortly after the British occupation, the German counter action was rapid. The enemy cannot have known that we were about to occupy Cos so that his preparation can have begun only after he learnt of the occupation.

Cos is a long, narrow island, 28 miles in length with an area of 109 square miles. Toward the South coast runs a limestone ridge rising above 1,600 feet for a distance of four or five miles, the highest peak being 2,800 ft. The population is or was, about 20,000, half of them inhabiting the town of Cos which has a small medieval harbour.

From the naval point of view Leros, with its numerous bays affording good harbours, is very much more important and had been by the Italians as a naval base.

GERMAN ON "MOPPING UP" IN COS

The German High Command report yesterday stated:

"On Sunday all sections of the German armed forces began a landing operation in the eastern Mediterranean against Cos. Enemy resistance was smashed and the island occupied in two days fighting. Six hundred men of the British garrison and 2,500 Badoglio troops were taken prisoner and 40 guns, 22 aircraft and one ship were captured. Mopping up of the last scattered enemy remnants on the island is in progress. – Reuter.

Reuter Agency 6 October

Still, on the **7 October 1943**:

"COS IN GERMAN HANDS"
ENEMY ACCOUNTING OF FIGHTING

The German wireless last night gave what it described as the first full account of the fighting for the island of Cos. The announcer said:

After Badoglio's betrayal the garrison of 3.000 men allowed a detachment of 1.000 British soldiers to land on the island to support them and take possession of the airfields. The Luftwaffe had, however, observed their operations and started heavy attacks on airfield installation and shipping, in the harbour of Leros two destroyers and several freighters were sunk and others damaged.

Early on Sunday morning a German naval formation of transports, landing craft and escort forces set out for Cos disembarking in the darkness at three points. The enemy, taken by surprise, opened heavy fire on the landing craft.

A little later airborne troops were landed in the western part of the island and fought against strong forces of the enemy, which advanced to meet them. After brief and violent fighting the resistance was everywhere broken. The Badoglio troops tried to take refuge in the mountains.

Supported by the Luftwaffe, German troops then undertook mopping-up operations against the British who tried to make a last stand. Altogether 3.100 prisoners including 600 British were taken. Our losses were only 15 killed and 70 wounded. The island of Cos, with its main town Kastron, and important airfields is to-day firmly in German hands.

German wireless last night reported heavy German air attack on Tuesday on Leros, the island in the Dodecanese, 40 miles north of Cos, which was occupied by British troops last month.

In spite of strong anti-aircraft opposition, said the wireless, the attack was carried out successfully. Several A.A. batteries being knocked out and two small ships were completely destroyed by bombs.

In Crete (or Candia), occupied by German troops, on October 6, two newspapers, "The Observer" and "The Voice of Crete" gave the news on the happening in Cos as follows:

THE GERMAN MILITARY LANDING SUCCEDED ON THE ISLAND OF COS

News from the Army

On October 3, the landing of German troops began in the eastern part of the Aegean Sea against the island of Kos, north of Rhodes. During the attacks the enemy resistance was broken and the island was occupied. 600 British soldiers and 2500 Badoglio's Army men were captured. 40 guns, 22 planes and a ship were captured. The mopping up of the free soldiers still continues.

In Italy, in Bari already freed by the allies, the Gazzetta del Mezzogiorno on October 7 recorded:

Cos Island

During the attack on the island of Coo, the Germans launched 2,000 paratroopers while other troops were landed. Allied troops, who added to the Italian garrison, are still resisting as allied aviation participates in the fight. But the Germans have already announced that they have occupied the island.

Anglo-American aviation bombed military targets in Rhodes and the island of Crete.

The "Corriere della Sera" information on October 8, from Milan, dominated by Nazi-fascists, in the context of the article: "The battle extends to the Velichi Luchi sector" refers to the news on Cos in the subtitle "Reinforce the Eighth Army":

Another dispatch from the Mediterranean front by Stefani's agency describes the landing action on the island of Cos made last October 3 by the Germans.

"The garrison - says the dispatch - made up of three thousand men from General Badoglio had facilitated the landing of British soldiers and put airports at their disposal for enemy aviation.

The German aviators, with continued flights to the island, could observe the enemy's movements passing the information to the Luftwaffe's command. Subsequently, the German air force began their attacks.

Massive bombings were carried out by Stuka against the landing fields, harbour and port facilities.

In one of these attacks, two destroyers were sunk and numerous transport vessels were damaged. After this preparation, in the early hours of Sunday morning, Germanic forces attacked. The grenadiers set foot on the island in three different points. The alarm had not yet occurred since many troops had engaged in the battle. Shortly thereafter, paratroopers came down on the island.

Having captured hundreds of prisoners, among them many British, German troops started raiding the island. Most of the garrison troop who fled into the mountains were captured after fierce fighting. "

The Battle reported by the Supplement to the London Gazette of Friday, 8th October, 1948

The following Despatch was submitted to the Lord Commissioners of the Admiralty on the 27th December, 1943, by Vice-Admiral Sir Algernon U. Willis, K.C.B., D.S.O., Commander in Chief Levant.

Levant

27th December, 1943

Be pleased to lay before Their Lordship the attached report of Naval Operations

in the Aegean between the 7th September, 1943 and 28th November , 1943
(Signed) A.U. Willis,
Vice-Admiral Commander in Chief.

Monday, 11 October, 1943
General report on Aegean operations
2....
3. Following our successful landing in Sicily with unexpectedly small losses of assault shipping and craft, an attempt was made to plan and mount "Accolade" using some forces as were available in the Middle East or were earmarked for India. Once again, it became necessary to call on Eisenhower to make up deficiencies, particularly in long range fighters, and, as a result, "Accolade" was cancelled by decision of the Combined Chiefs of Staff, at the Quadrant Conference[17]. The Commander in Chief, Middle East informed the Chiefs of Staff on 31st August that the only operations which could be mounted from Middle East were:
(a) Small Scale Raids.
(b) Sabotage and Guerrilla operations by Resistance Groups.
(c) Unopposed "walk in" to areas evacuated by the enemy.

Phase I
Surrender of Italy to the opening of the German Air offensive
8th to 26th September, 1943
4. When it was known that Italy had surrender, it was decided to take advantage at this situation by encouraging the Italian garrisons to hold such Aegean island as they could against the Germans, and to stiffen their resistance by sending in small parties of British troops. Between 8th and 16th September, Casteloriso, Kos, Leros, Samos, Kalimnos, Symi, Stampalia were all occupied by small detachments of Raiding Force troops accompanied by Civil Affairs Officers. Fairmile motor launches and caiques of the Levant Schooner Flotilla manned by the Royal Naval crews provided the transport.
5. In Rhodes our emissaries were unable to prevent the Italian Governor surrendering the island to the Germans after a short resistance. (There were 30.000 Italian and 7.000 German troops in the island) The combined service mission waiting at Casteloriso and the 234 Infantry Brigade waiting to proceed to Rhodes were therefore held available to reinforce the British force in the other islands.
......
9. Prior to the Italian surrender, the Germans had made preparations to take over the entire military administration of Greece as from the 6th September and had disposed sufficient forces on the West coast of Greece, the Peloponnesus, Melos, Crete, Scarpanto, and Rhodes, to ensure the retention of their control in these key positions.

---

[17] *Admiralty footnote:* Quadrant Conference – the British-American conference held at Quebec in August, 1943

In the period immediately following the surrender, the Germans were in no positions to undertake seaborne operations, owing to the lack of shipping, escort vessel and landing craft, which they had to obtain from the Italians or transfer from other areas. By the middle of September, however, they had collected enough craft to despatch raiding forces to the Cyclades to evacuate the Italian garisson and such food and war material as they could lay their hands on. With the exception of Syra they established observation posts only and did not garrison the islands in force.

10. Apart from Rhodes, the Italians' attitude was co-operative in the islands visited by us, though their fighting value was low. It was considered that even if Leros were reinforced by such British troops as were available and Kos airfields developed and defended adequately, we should not be in a secure position to continue operations in the Aegean until Rhodes was in our possession.

Accordingly on 22nd September the Chiefs of Staff approval was obtained to mount "Accolade" before the end of October with such forces as were available in the Middle east and could be spared from the Central Mediterranean.

Phase II
The Start of the German Offensive.
26th September – 12th October

11. With the arrival of large enemy air reinforcement from France and the Russian front and the proved inefficiency of the A.A. defence of Leros, as shown by the sinking of H.M.S. Intrepid and H.M.S. Queen Olga in Leros harbour on the 26th September, operations of our surface forces in the Aegean were restricted to sweep during the dark hours with forces who retired to the south-eastward to obtain fighter cover from Cyprus during the day. On 1st October all available Fleet destroyers were sailed to Malta as escort to H.M. Ships Howe and King George , leaving us with the Hunts whose speed and endurance made it difficult for them to operate far into the Aegean and still be clear by daylight. As result, H.M.S. Aldenhan, H.H.M.S. Miaoulis and H.H.M.S. Themistocles who were patrolling off Kaso Strait o the night of the 2nd / 3rd October, were short of fuel and in no position to take action on an aircraft report of an enemy convoy sighted off Naxos and believed on all available intelligence to be bound to Rhodes. They were ordered to withdraw to Alexandria for fuel. This convoy, in fact, carried an invasion force which was landed on Cos at 0500 on October 3rd and captured the island in spite of stubborn resistance from the British battalion, who received small assistance from the Italian garrison.

12. No surface forces was available to interfere with the landing, but submarines on patrol were ordered to proceed to the Cos area to attack invasion shipping.............

15. *It now became apparent that our forces could not enter the Aegean to intercept enemy shipping and be clear again by daylight, and that further attempts would lead to unacceptable losses, more especially as the Lightning Squadrons were withdrawn to the Central Mediterranean. Accordingly the policy was adopted of operating destroyers only as an anti-invasion force, and using cruisers to provide A.A. and fighter direction during approach and retirement from the Aegean and for operations in such areas they could reach during the night.*

16. *The loss of Cos airfields, besides finally destroying our hopes of fighter cover for our surface forces, greatly increased the difficulties of supply as it prevented the passage and unloading of merchant ships and heavy lift ships which were urgently required to provide heavy A.A. defences and to improve the transport situation in Leros. The capture of Rhodes became increasingly important for the continuation of our operations.*

17. *On 9th October, a meeting was held at Tunis, attended by General Eisenhower, the First Sea Lord and all Commanders-in-Chief in the Mediterranean and Middle East, including the Commander-in-chief, Levant, Admiral Sir John H.D. Cunningham to consider the situation and it was finally decided that our resources would not allow us to mount Operation "Accolade", but they should try to hold Leros and Samos as long as supplies could be maintained.*

....

Conclusion

78. *These operations were carried out to take advantage of the Italian surrender to obtain a foothold in the Aegean with such forces as were available in the Middle East. We failed because we were unable to establish airfields in the area of operations.*

79. *The enemy's command of the air enabled him so to limit the operations and impair the efficiency of land, sea and air forces that by picking his time he could deploy his comparatively small forces with decisive results.*

80. *The naval forces engaged on these operations, cruisers, destroyers, submarines and coastal craft, and the small force of aircraft available to 201 (Naval Co-operation) Group all fought hard and did valiant work under particularly trying conditions. They achieved considerably success against the enemy and held off the attack on Leros for some time, but not without heavy casualties to our own forces.*

81. *Had more aircraft been available, especially modern long range fighters, and given more luck, the operations might have been prolonged, but after the loss of Cos, if the enemy was prepared to divert the necessary effort, it is doubtful if Leros could have been held indefinitely without embarking on a major operation for which no forces were available.*

82. *It may be, however, that the inroad made in the enemy shipping's resources – which prove a fatal handicap to him when the time comes for us to embark on an "all in" offensive in the Aegean, with adequate forces.*

꓾umb. 38426

5371

SUPPLEMENT TO

The London Gazette

OF FRIDAY, 8th OCTOBER, 1948

𝔓𝔲𝔟𝔩𝔦𝔰𝔥𝔢𝔡 𝔟𝔶 𝔄𝔲𝔱𝔥𝔬𝔯𝔦𝔱𝔶

Registered as a newspaper

MONDAY, 11 OCTOBER, 1948

NAVAL OPERATIONS IN THE AEGEAN BETWEEN THE
7TH SEPTEMBER, 1943 AND 28TH NOVEMBER, 1943.

The following Despatch was submitted to the   3. Following our successful landings in Sicily

GERMAN OCCUPATION CONSEQUENCES

The Italian Army Officers' Disappearance

The British prisoners, about 900, were assembled at the Carabinieri Office housed in the Governor's Palace. They were treated according to their status as Prisoners of War.

The Italian prisoners, almost 3,000, were herded into the Knights Castle. They suffered maltreatment, hunger and all kinds of cruelty. Many of them were killed on the slightest pretext/provocation. One was shot because, having received permission to go to piss, returned mistakenly to another place.

A few went over to the side of the Germans, hoping for better treatment. Some, during the night, jumped from the high wall of the castle to escape with the help of some Greeks; others, able to escape, boarded boats in the harbour, trying to hide themselves under the sand the boats were transporting. A number died doing this.

The Italian officers where massed in the same castle; then transferred to a barracks at Linopoti, almost 13 kms West on the main road Cos Kefalo.

On the island, in those days, there were 148 Army Italian Officers all listed by father Michelangelo Bacheca, the catholic priest, who remained in Cos until the liberation from the German occupation. Only 7 collaborated with the Germans, others were spared since they

The Knights Castle- Cos [18]

---

[18] Photos and drawings on pag 186 are supplied by Vasilis S. Hatzivasileiou, historic and lawyer of Cos. His work translated into English by Professor Nicholas G. Itsines is: *"History of the island of Kos"* pages 729 – published on 2013 by The Municipality of Kos

were non-combatant officers like doctors, chaplains, administration officers.

In the days following capture, between October the 4th to the 7th, 103 officers were executed in a field, following a disgraceful charade of a military hearing. 84 of them were under 28 years of age. Their bodies were put in 8 mass graves.

Almost a year later a collaborating lieutenant, in the absence of Captain Nasca, a fascist co-operating with the Germans, convinced a newly posted German Commander, Maj Heinemeir, to search for the graves in Ciclicà, next to the salty plain (Salina), to counter the rumours circulating on the island as to the true fate of the Italian officers. They were supposed to have been transported to the continent to German Prison camps.

The graves were found, excavated and 66 bodies counted. Only 42 of them were recognized by their personal belongings or documents. The other 37 bodies were never found. There are people who know where the killing of the remaining officers took place. A search by metal detectors in such defined areas in Lambi and in the salty plain could have been possible in those days.

The 66 bodies were transported in October 1944 to the Catholic Cemetery in Cos and in 1954 transferred to the Military Ossuary in Bari where they now rest in peace[19].

Only in recent years, in 1992, a memorial stone has been erected in the catholic cemetery in Cos by the Aegean Veterans and the Municipality of the town. For years a lady, Helene Klonari, has voluntarily taken on the task of tending this tombstone, the small Italian Cemetery and explaining to visitors what did happen to the officers listed on the tombstone.

On a small marble plaque it is written: " *We remember with sadness and mourning the Italian officers slaughtered by the German Nazis*". The

---

[19] The military chaplain, Don Luigi Ghilardini, who was tasked to transport to Italy the remains of the Acqui division's Fallen from the island of Kefalonia, was charged with the exhumation of the Cos remains from the common burial in the Catholic cemetery of Cos and fetch them to the Homeland. Such operation was carried out from the 24th to the 26th May, 1954.

plate was placed over there by a German pastor but in the writing he made an error: the slaughter was committed not by German Nazis but by German soldiers of the Wehrmacht.

Cos is known by the Aegean veterans and their families as *the little Kefalonia*"; the term refers not to the extension of the island but to the number of Italian officers murdered after capture. They were, and still are, considered traitors. To this day, the German Judicial System still considers as such these murdered officers, although General Telford Taylor's declared in his summing-up at the Nuremberg War Trial:

"This calculated slaughter of captured or surrendered Italian officers is one of the most lawless and dishonourable actions in the long history of armed combat. For these men were fully uniformed. They bore their arms openly and followed the rules and customs of war. They were led by responsible leaders who, in repelling attack, were obeying the orders of Marshall (Pietro) Badoglio, their military commander in chief and the duly authorized political head of their nation. They were regular soldiers entitled to respect, human consideration, and chivalrous treatment."

These words were directed to General Lange, CO of the XXII Army Corps operating in Epirus. One of the accusations was *"… the troops under his command and jurisdiction to execute the captured Italian General Gandin, CO of the Acqui Division, and all officers of his staff"*.

At that time no one fully knew what was done in Kefalonia by the German troops. [20]

3,800 men were killed in mass shootings, put on fire and then, since the bodies didn't turn to ashes, sunk in wells from where some years later the remains were transported into the Military Cemetery in Bari. To this day, Kefalonian and Ithican villagers when they see a column of smoke, say: *"The souls of the Acqui Division Soldier's are going up to the sky."*

Out of 525 Italian Officers on Kefalonia:
- 65 were killed during the fighting
- 189 were shot on the spot when found

[20] The Lost Sons of The Mediterranean – Kefalonia – September 1943 : by Pietro Giovanni Liuzzi – Editor : youcanprint self-publishing - Italia- 2014

- 136 were shot at the Red House after they had surrendered. Bodies were weighed-down and sunk in the sea. 8 Italian sailors used to transport the bodies from the killing field to the shore and then on a boat which was later taken by a tug to the open sea and then sunk, were ordered to excavate a big hole, then they too, were shot and buried so there were no witnesses.

- 135 were spared and sent to prison camps in Germany

Captain Pampaloni, the one assumed to be the character of Captain Corelli in the De Bernieres' novel, used to say: *War is terrible. I have spent my life to make propaganda for peace".*

Mr. Bensi, the secretary of the Aegean civilian and military veterans, during the dedication of the Memorial tombstone in the catholic cemetery in Cos said:

"... being our hearts heavily sad for the gravity of that crime committed without justification, we limit ourselves in praying and hoping that the remorse touches the consciences of the responsible still alive and drive their sons or nephews, perhaps not unaware of that folly, to bend their heads and ask God what we cannot concede".

A marble plate placed by Father Michelangelo Bacheca at the foot of the mass grave in the Catholic Cemetery says:

"Piously extracted from the graves in Linopoti, here rest since March 1945 the mortal remains of 66 out of more than 100 Italian officers clandestinely killed by the German machine guns in October 1943".

The Officer's Killing

Stephen Roskill in his book *The war at sea* writes «[...] *True to the Nazi habit of wreaking cruel vengeance, the victor at once shot ninety Italian officers* [...].

It was the morning of October 5, 1943. Arghiri Puglia [21] with other boys was playing with a ball of rags in Rotunda Square. All that space

---

[21] Cos citizen, he was 14 when he left the island immediately after the German occupation. He served as a waiter in the Officer's Mess in Palestine. Two years later he was enrolled in the British Police at Symi. With his family he moved to Italy where he lives in Latina town, see reference page 53 Archive references

was just for them and they could enjoy it completely without fear of bothering anyone.

Suddenly the boys heard the sound of footsteps growing ever louder and their attention was drawn to the direction the sound came from. It was a group of soldiers who proceeded in a "broken" step, and as the platoon approached, they recognized them: they were Italian officers. They walked quietly, three were staggering, escorted by German soldiers. Arghiri cannot say how many there were because he did not feel necessary to count them; maybe eighty. They headed out of town to Platani (better known as Ghermè) and Linopoti. He recognized a major, he was one of those who, when the fall of Fascism was revealed, went around the city with some of his soldiers to destroy the relevant symbols. The boys thought of their transfer to another prison camp; they did not bother and started playing again.

Only after his return from Palestine Arghiri learned from the Superior Mother of Cos Hospital, which end was reserved for that group of Italians: they were all killed in the watershed of Ciflicà near Linopoti.

Toward the early months of 1944, the rumour that the officers escorted to the Salina had been killed there was confirmed by the discovery of human remains buried in the land where some farmers were plowing and by some soldiers of the Working Company [22] who on the 5th, 6th and 7th of October 1943 excavated suspect graves at Ciflicà

It was April 24, 1944, a Pillis' shepherd who had noticed tracts of earth in a scarcely frequented area at Marmari, informed Padre Sportoletti, chaplain of the 10th Regiment. He decided to carry out an immediate reconnaissance of the area described. When he arrived in the area, with some workers, he went into the vegetation and reached a grassy field in the middle of which a section of land appeared to be loose. A few shovels were needed to find the bodies covered with mud. At this point, the survey ended: it was necessary to ask and wait

---

[22] Workers' Company : prisoners employed in activities ordered by the Germans

for the German Command's permission before removing the bodies and transferring them to a common grave in the Catholic cemetery.

(Gianazzi) [23] *An act of courage was the identification of the Linopoti pits, containing the remains of Italian officers assassinated after the German's landing. This was possible because, taking advantage of Captain Nasca's absence, his vice, Lieutenant Enzo Aiello, was able to get permission from the German Command. In fact he reported protests by islanders and Italian soldiers, according to which, after the landing and occupation of Cos, the massacre of over a hundred Italian officers was conducted. To silence rumours and avoid problems during a period of limited presence of German soldiers, he asked for and obtained permission for carrying out an inspection in the Linopoti bush. 66 officers were exhumed receiving worthy and honoured burial in the Catholic cemetery of Cos.*

Some days later Lieutenant Aiello was denounced by Captain Nasca to the German Military Tribunal for insubordination. The officer would have been sentenced if the Germans had not surrendered in 1945.

(Father Bacheca) *The criterion that determined the designation of the victims was confirmed: it was depending upon whether or not the role anyone had during the fight, did he participate so to be held accountable for the events, or rather the resistance? There was no process, not defence, but only the determination of the military, as evidenced by the testimonies of those concerned and, perhaps, by some designation, if not indiscretion, of colleagues.*

Executions began on the evening of October 4, with the shooting of the commander of the island, Colonel Leggio Felice, and some of his main and most direct co-adjutants. The killings ended at dawn of the 7th October, on which day, the various local testimonies, as far as they know, agree to fix the most significant number of victims. However, it is certain that a few isolated executions took place in the following days.

The suppression was aimed at the officers. This is proven not only with the positive results obtained in the exploration of the pits and the German

---

[23] The Surname in brackets refer to the author of the reported writing

admissions, but also with the criterion of responsibility that led to that accusation.

On the 5th and 6th of October, the captured officers were judged by order of the the division's Commander, General Friedrich Wilhelm Müller. In the two concentration centres, an infantry lieutenant, whose name is unknown, and a captain acted as inquirers. During the course of the trial there were some episodes of true courage:

- Lieutenant Coratza Salvatore, flag bearer of the regiment, faced the dilemma to reveal the place where the flag of the 10th Regiment was hidden or to be killed, the ultimate solution, he accepted to sacrifice his life.
- Lieutenant De Giovanni repeatedly invited all officers and soldiers of his sector to identify him for being responsible for the long-lasting resistance.
- The subordinates Stracuzzi and Ferrera spontaneously declared to the German officer that they forced their commander to resist and open fire against the enemy. They saved him by sacrificing their two young lives.

The process was done with the utmost lightness. Captain Kulmann was at Kamari, outdoors, assisted by an interpreter (a certain Joseph of Bolzano) who knew very little Italian. The Italian officers were called one at a time and submitted to a few questions, then divided into two groups. During the time long enough to smoke a cigarette, 16 officers were condemned. The same thing happened in Linopoti.

1. - 40 officers identified by strictly personal documents or objects. Are the following:

Lt Col	Baldacchino Carlo	Lieut	Capparuccia Filippo
Maj	Simone Riccardo	2 Lieut	Ardito Luigi
Capt	Burana Egidio	2 Lieut	Aresu Giorgio
Capt	De Flaviis Ettore	2 Lieut	Auricchio Gennaro
Capt.	Li Mandri Vincenzo	2 Lieut	Battegazzore Andrea
Capt	Rovelli Giuseppe	2 Lieut	Bondanelli Luigi
Capt	Scotti Emilio	2 Lieut	Bonelli Fernando
Capt	Terruggia Giovanni	2 Lieut	Bosio Franco
Lieut	Anselmi Antonio	2 Lieut	Bruatti Fortunato
Lieut	Cacciari Emilio	2 Lieut	Vagliasindi G.
Lieut	Cardinale Vincenzo	2 Lieut	Carrieri Aldo
Lieut	Coratza Salvatore	2 Lieut	Custodero Francesco
Lieut	D'Alessandro Ettore	2 Lieut	Ferrera Pietro
Lieut	Trinastich Giovanni	2 Lieut	Lo Piano Francesco
Lieut	Lettieri Antonio	2 Lieut	Nocera Gaspare

Lieut	Marongiu Alberto	2 Lieut	Pinto Vincenzo
Lieut	Menegatti Gino	2 Lieut	Silvestri Bruno
Lieut	Picardi Luigi	2 Lieut	Stracuzzi Cesare
Lieut	Rotella Francesco	2 Lieut	Fiadino Matteo

2. - 46 officers and 1 NCO whose death is alleged because there was no positive evidence of documents, clothing, objects, etc.

Col	Leggio Felice	2 Lieut	Capecchi Giuseppe
Lt Col	Bonserio Francesco	2 Lieut	Caruso Giuseppe
Lt Col	Castrogiovanni Vinc.	2 Lieut	Casella Mario
Capt	Boschi Aldo	2 Lieut	Comotti Ugo
Capt	Colussi Giovanbattista	2 Lieut	D'Orsi Gaetano
Capt	Costadoni Mario	2 Lieut	Elefante Gioacchino
Capt	Fiorentini Aldo	2 Lieut	Esposito Gennaro
Capt.	Olivieri Giovanni	2 Lieut	Lorusso Michele
Capt	Rizzoli Guido	2 Lieut	Mainardis Mariano
Cap	Zaffagnini Enrico	2 Lieut	Mancini Giovanni
Lieut	Cappelli Vincenzo A.	2 Lieut	Mariani Enzo
Lieut	Di Tommaso Antonio	2 Lieut	Marino Prospero
Lieut	Fossari Bernardino	2 Lieut	Monachesi Remo
Lieut	Massa Stefano	2 Lieut	Petruni Domenico
Lieut	Pizzicaroli Luigi	2 Lieut	Poggiani Pietro
Lieut	Sardelli Dario	2 Lieut	Quaranta Pietro
Lieut	Brignone Raffaele	2 Lieut	Viti Livio
Lieut	Scarvaglieri Vito	2 Lieut	Rea Eleuterio
Lieut	Velasquez Angelo	2 Lieut	Rossi Raffaele
Lieut	Zaddei Carlo	2 Lieut	Somaini Giovanni
2 Lieut	Azzaro Francesco	2 Lieut	Talbi Vincenzo
2 Lieut	Bellomo Rosario	2 Lieut	Valletta Francesco
2 Lieut	Bosna Alfredo	NCO	Falaschi Olimpo
2 Lieut	Busi Luciano		

3. - 9 Officers whose death is likely to be counted by some testimony. Such is the case of Colaprico, who was a canteen officer and Lieutenant Caminiti, a veterinarian of the regiment. The 9 are the following:

Maj	Paola Luigi	2 Lieut	Caminiti Nicola
Lieut	Bianca Ennio	2 Lieut	D'Amore Michele
Lieut	Colaprico Leon.	2 Lieut	Frezza Giuseppe
Lieut	Citro Salvatore	2 Lieut	Vezzosi Filippo
Lieut	Lupone Federico		

So there are 96 names on the list of the victims found, albeit with varying degrees. I do not rule out a mistake. God wanted my suppositions to be all a mistake. I'm afraid that, if there is any mistake, it will be minimal.

On the epigraph of the tomb that holds those sacred mortal remains, I wrote "the majority of a hundred ". Was that figure crazy? It would seem yes. But it is not so. That is the number recorded in the Book of the Dead of my parish Agnus Dei. There are other names in discussion.

There is, first of all, the case of heroic Lieutenant De Giovanni. The brave officer was certainly imprisoned in the Linopoti concentration camp, he managed to escape; he hid himself in Kefalos, where he left in mid October. But it is also certain that in the pits was discovered his cigarette case, from which, according to the testimony of those who knew him intimately, it was not easy to separate from him, though he was not a big smoker. There is no news of him from the unlucky October. How is the mystery explained? He was perhaps captured again by the Germans, or during the fleeing to sea from Kefalos, or because he was betrayed by persons who helped him to flee to steal, perhaps, the large sum of money he carried with him and the Germans brought him back and destined to perish among the first? The hypothesis would very well reconcile the two facts that seem contradictory, certain escape from Linopoti and the presence of his body in the pits due to the discovery of the cigarette case. The De Giovanni case is very complex. But its end now is tempting to doubt, it is evident that the number of victims of our tragedy rises to 97.

There is the case of the artillery major, anonymous for the moment [24], coming from Rhodes where he commanded a battery and where he had fled due to the events of that island. On 3 October he was certainly on Cos; different persons attest to his presence among the prisoners passing through the streets of the city and then picked up at Linopoti. With him, therefore, 98 would be the victims.

Finally, there are 8 other names for which no news has been collected.

The slaughter of our officers appears true and concrete in the etymological sense of the word. The sacrifice of hundreds of our officers, if it is not adequately appreciated by men, often too easily forgotten, is atoned before God for our Country and for this Island, even though the blood that they poured out in it has not been sufficient to preserve it to the Homeland.

---

[24] Major Da Vià Vito. He is one of the five officers out of 103 awarded with the Silver Medal

Papateodorakis' house ruins

Big tree placed in front of the "Graves' Field"

Forked tree in the Graves' Field

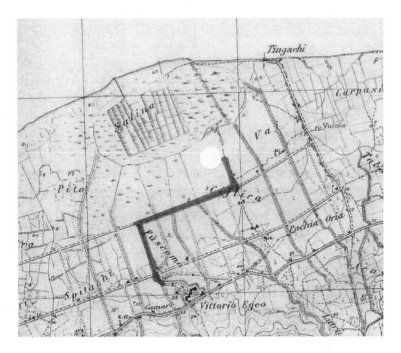

The path from the Barracks "Vittorio Egeo" to the Graves'Field
Tavoletta al 25000 of IGM - Asfendiu.

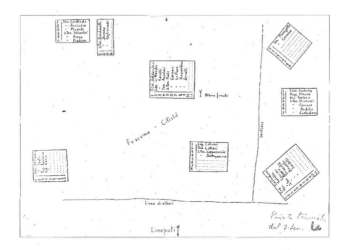

The Aiello's map and the 8 common graves

To reach the Graves' Field: from Cos, after Zibàri, turn right to Tingachi and then, at the second crossroads, to the left via Capodistria to Marmari. Overtaking the Blue Sky Hotel the ruin of Papateodorakis's house are visible. The right-hand side road leads to Salina. After Georgeos Matteos's home there is a large tree on the left, beyond which is the Graves' Field with the forked tree.

115

Attempts for the surrender of Lieut. De Giovanni

The capture

(Squeo) *The Germans vent their lower instincts of race. In the dormitories all the military boxes were broken and the objects they contained were removed. Everything was taken away from my room: personal kit, blankets, linen, uniforms, shoes, camera, 12,000 lire in banknotes and my spare lenses were crushed under their feet only for pure evil. The soldier's wrists watches were robbed and to those very few reluctant were pointed with the pistols.*

My artillerymen were directed to a gathering place while Lieutenant Poggiani and I were taken to a shepherd's house where a German company command had been set up. I found a dozen Italian officers captured before me, including Lieutenant Colonel Castrogiovanni, Captain Cibeu (commander of the 246th battery), Lieutenant Stracuzzi, Lieutenant Lovero and others who I do not remember the names of. As soon as I got inside, my coat was taken away from me with violence to cover a German wounded. I stayed in shorts, shirt and sandals, having had no time, that tragic morning, to wear the uniform.

I was pushed into the cottage with the epithets of "coward, traitor", and so on and in bad Italian we were told none of us would come out alive because for each wounded German soldier an Italian would have been slain adopting the Russian system.

In the afternoon I was first brought out and questioned by an angry-looking German captain: Kuhlmann. He told me, through an interpreter, that my behaviour had been rebellious and that, after three years war as allied, I should not have given orders to shoot against the Germans.

He wanted to know why I had given orders to resist. I replied that, like him, I was a soldier and as such I did not have to discuss the orders received. My situation, in this summary process, worsened with the intervention of a parachutist officer who arrived at that moment, who told his colleague that he had no pity for me because I had fired against his men whilst descending in the air. The process was over. The German captain, mounted on all the rage, made me saying I was "a pig and a coward". He called a soldier, ordered him to charge the machine gun, and wanted me to go to the nearby ridge. My fellow prisoners were called to attend the scene.

Slowly, I started toward the ridge, where capital execution would have to take place. I was lucky since the captain was urgently called by his radio operator station where he read a phonogram. Gave some orders and quickly walked away from his soldiers with the command gear. I was brought back to the lodge and put together with my colleagues.

On the evening of October 3, the situation was disastrous for us. About ¾ of the island, including Antimachia's landing ground had fallen into German hands. In this area there were three antiaircrafts batteries {62nd, 63rd, 64th}, the 74/27 {246th}, my battery the 149/12 {136th}, infantry units and a contingent of allied troops stationed in the Landing ground (D Coy). No news on the fate of Cos' sector. I stayed in the lodge with the other officers until late night. My health was worrying me, I had high temperature which increased my state of frustration and general moral downfall.

The surrender invitation

That evening, late in the night, a German paratrooper officer appeared into the lodge. In bad Italian, he ordered me to go with one of their NCOs to the 12th infantry company (Lieutenant De Giovanni) to convince him and his men to surrender.

This mission was entrusted to me in the presence of captured Italian officers, including Lieutenant Colonel Castrogiovanni, who personally encouraged me. I was handed over to an NCO.

After two hour walking, during which I was constantly threatened, the German told me to proceed alone whilst he would have followed me and controlled at a short distance. As soon as I was near the company's barbed wire entanglement, I was under fire. I tried to identify myself shouting my rank and name. Being recognised I managed to cross the netting and, finally, I met Lieutenant De Giovanni.

Having told all the events I had incurred, I passed on to him the message. He assured me with immense joy that at 0400 next morning substantial allied forces would have arrived in the bay of Kamari from Leros, Cyprus and Alexandria. Lieutenant De Giovanni was in radio contact with Leros. I heartened and hoped I could repay back to the German counterpart the same treatment I had received.

Before leaving for my return, I greeted for good luck my collegue, assuring him my mission would not have the results as the Germans hoped. We exchanged a hug and I started off on the way back with the German NCO awaiting for me over the barbed wire line.

My mission, therefore, had to be related to the time De Giovanni wanted to earn and the outcome of my task. I had the lucky intuition to report to the German lieutenant I had not been recognized by the company commander in the way I was dressed and due to my general conditions. Moreover he had been replaced in the last days and he refused the encounter because we didn't know each other.

Such a version obviously did not persuade the German so he sent someone to fetch Lieutenant Colonel Castrogiovanni. He arrived at about 0200 and when I met him I had the chance to brief him on what had happened to me. After a while the colonel was introduced to the German lieutenant and, some time later, a letter was handed to me to be delivered to the 12th Company Commander. I realized my lie had been accepted for truth but it would be impossible to repeat the same ploy for a second time.

I was tasked with this second mission. I had the obligation to return not a minute later than 0600 o'clock in the same morning. So I was sure that the Germans, awaiting for my answer, would not have attacked. I set out hoping to pick up a weapon and return to the place with some of the announced reinforcements.

At first I told Lieutenant De Giovanni not to take into account the letter that had been written for the sole purpose of gaining time. However time was passing by without receiving news on the reinforcement. I had to go back for that fixed hour also because I had to save the other officers in hostage having a negative message of no surrender. There were moments of spasmodic waiting and of atrocious disappointments, while the spirit of our duty in all of us was growing even greater. I was still in the middle of the barbed wire entanglement when German airplanes flew over our heads and many paratroopers had been seen coming on the ground.

Once they touched the ground in conjunction with automatic weapons and tank units already displayed on the previous day, a bloody battle lit up. Even this time, the superiority of men and weapons, tanks and airplanes, was favourable for the Germans. I was isolated, 200 yards away from De Giovanni's first positions. I was re-captured and put together with the other prisoners.

In the afternoon of the same day (4.10.43) we knew that the entire island had been occupied by the Germans. The next day, some of the prisoners were sent to Cos and some to the Antimachia Landing Ground.

Terror, violence, and arbitrariness

"The occupation of Cos by the Alemanian troops was a matter of only two days, but the whole life of the island was upset. For about twenty months, terror, violence, and arbitrariness reigned." With these words Father Michelangelo Bacheca describes in a memorial what was happening in those days on that island. And he goes on: *"We should not talk of looting as a continuum factor, because this sad inherence due to any violent occupation of war should be resolved within a few days. Instead, in Cos it became a system.*

It begun by the nude and hungry assault troops, dropped down from the sky on the island, possessed by that abominable and eminently destructive method that history has set as its own and exclusive to the Germanic invasions of every era. It stopped only with the English occupation. No house, no shop, no public building was spared. Food, money, precious objects, wools, women's clothing were systematically taken without regard and unconsciously destroyed and dispersed. The wider, though, and, by far, more damaging than the soldier was the looting we call official.

The adjective will appear more than just as soon as it is known that for this purpose they had created a special warehouse and store, in Lambi, guarded by a lame official. From October 5 onwards, seaplanes apparently sent for this purpose, arrived at Cos, preferring to the "CAIR"docks (Italian Agricultural Rhodes Consortium) and carrying loads of all kinds of objects, furniture, garments, carpets, household and office equipment, taken away from private houses that the owners had been forced to abandon and from public offices. Various sailing and motor boats were also destined for such a need.

One of the latter, departing from the dock on October 20, loaded with furniture and household goods of all kinds taken largely from the Palace of the Delegation, was sunk off Cos and Calimno, and for a few days floating on the sea were seen parts of them.

Terror, which apparently is the essential element of the much-proclaimed German value, was vast in the first months and never ceased completely. It is sadly true because episodes of ferocity and brutality were told by everyone, perhaps exaggerating and widening, as unfortunately happens in such contingencies. Unfortunately, it is true that the Germans threw bombs at random in trenches and specially in shelters without knowing if soldiers or civilians were in them.

It is an established and documented fact that Italian farmer Eugenio Lovari on October 7 was shot on the doorstep of his house while attempting to rescue his wife from sexual violence. This crime impressed the settlers of the Linopoti farm company to oblige them to leave their homes completely.

Many captured prisoners attested that a prisoner in Antimachia camp was made to run to be the macabre target of some NCOs pistols, others said officers.

The corpse of a man, a prisoner at the castle, called to be a part of a bunch of workers, was killed on the spot only because, having asked permission to get some privacy to satisfy a natural need returned to another place because he was lost. His body was buried a few centimeters under the ground,

A hand grenade was thrown against muslim Mustafa Mislì because he was trying to avoid the robbery of his livestock. The German Command had issued him a document authorizing him for not to surrender anymore animals considering he had given already enough.

An old woman was killed by a guardian soldier while trying to collect in the slaughterhouse some offals to feed herself.

How many of these brutality? Impossible and out of place to review them all.

Father Michelangelo mentions the many carnal violence, the

carelessness, the exclusion of civilians from anti-aircraft shelters, the transfer of only German wounded to safe place, thefts of furniture and surgical material from the Linopoti Hospital, just before a violent naval bombardment hit Cos town.

[...] Italian prisoners suffered hunger and were subjected to the toughest jobs and despite the huge war booty that the Germans had made including invaluable quantities of food, that passed on to the prisoners of the castle consisted only of a tablespoon of sugar and a fistful of pasta that was eaten raw when there was no chance of cooking it. [...] "And then" *[...] It is a fundamental rule of all the armies, to respect the defeated since they become untouchable and sacred. But the invaders did not want to hear this even the sense of humanity and slaughtered the survivors who are now in vain, with cynicism and cruelty that has no precedent in the history of any civilian people.* "

British prisoners. Picture from: *"The Battle of Kos".*

Doctor Zervanos Giovanni's buildings at Platis Potamos
used by the *Feldgendarmerie Commandatur* - 1943 up to '45

Dimitris Tripolitis, at that time a 20-year-old Greek witness, points out that German soldiers were also violent among themselves. He tells that a member of the Military Police (Feldgendarmerie) was in an inn; somewhat drunk, he did not want to stop drinking. Soon afterward he was approached by one of his companions who invited him to leave the shop. He reacted firing at the newcomer with no hesitation.

And it is still Dimitris who mentions the robberies suffered by his father, a wealthy merchant with two nearby stores and well stocked in one of the main streets of the town. In one shop there were textiles and in the next one there was an exposition of glassware. The German soldiers had already loaded all the available cloths on the trucks and were beginning to empty the other room at the orders of a police captain who, with a whiplash, dropped objects that were not of his favour placed in the jambs. *"Why do you destroy what you do not need. By selling those items I can feed my family"* exclaimed his father. The captain approached him. He took with one hand his throat and with the other he aimed his pistol at his head. It was then that the poor man with contempt said: *"This is a shameful behaviour that does not adhere to a German officer."* The captain, after a few seconds, loosened his grip. He signaled to his soldiers and went out without speaking.

Dimitris is a quiet person, he knows many languages, and lends himself with obvious courtesy to a tour of the city to show where the officers' palaces are, the entrance to the sports' field, and all those buildings whose images have been already portrayed. Showing a window, he says, *"General Müller came out from there. One day some German soldiers came to our farmhouse to pick up my father. In the family we were all terrified; we wondered what they had accused him of. When they left, I followed them. They took him to their command to inform him that in our home in town General Müller would have stayed for a few days. Of course, at the news, we all breathed a sigh of relief at home. Our concerns were more."*

Passing the Mosque in the market square, Dimitris, somewhat saddened, shows me the tree to which a shepherd was hanged. *"One morning, the German military forced the citizens out of their houses and* gathered them in the main square," he says. "People wondered what had happened so important. Then, suddenly, the crowd of people squinted at the sound of a long roll of drums; marking the footstep of armed soldiers' platoon escorting a terrified man. He was a 50-year-old old shepherd who, gathering branches of bushes in a field, saw a cable lying on the ground. He cut a piece of it to tie the pile of branches. Unfortunately he did not know that it was part of a telephone line. The Germans captured and condemned him with the charge of sabotage. This is why he was there, in front of us with a sign hanging on his neck and standing on a chair having his hands tied behind his back. He was so scared that he did not speak.

"The III Reich traitors are punished in this way." It was written on the sign. Nearby there was one of the working company Italian soldier; he was ordered to pull the rope tied to the chair. Incredulous, the soldier resisted opposing a rigid refusal despite knowing the risk he was running into. It was then that a German soldier, angrily, clutched the rope and gave it a tug. "

The Mosque   The ancient wall   The marble plate

To the right of the mosque [25] there is a mulberry tree and behind, the castle wall and on a spot of it the marble plate remembering: *"Ilia Kapiri - Hanged by the Germans - on 28.11.43"*.

The following is the 3rd part of the report by Carlo Gianazzi, very significant and cruel. It refers to the period October 5, 1943 - May 9, 1945 issued to the Commission for the Italian Interest Protection in the Dodecanese on September 27, 1945.

---

[25] the minaret was destroyed in the recent earthquake that struck Kos in July 2017

This is the period of major suffering for Italians, both military and civilians, during which all kinds of violence was acted: insult, robbery, hunger and beatings have been endured with the specter of death always lurking. The mass of prisoners was transported to Greece, some hundred remained in Cos in slavery. Tearful and hungry workers obliged to carry out heavy tasks were subjected to fierce persecution if unwilling to join the Germanic armed forces. The weakest and the sick, to whom medical cure was even denied, perished.

The causes that slowed down physical and moral resistance prisoners' capacity, causing them to meditate coldly advantageous opportunities for escape and struggle, were due to the news of the sinking of ships carrying prisoners to the continent, the prohibition to corresponde to anyone or receiving civil aids, the exposition night and day at the risk of air and naval bombardment, without clothing, without a bed but naked soil. By contrast, the example and the exhortation of some disbelievers who at first had deployed decisively on the part of the enemy (Captain Camillo Nasca and Centurion Michele Tetro). Thus, the surviving prisoners adhered to the German armed forces as fighters and workers, and it was not long afterwards that the atmosphere of "camaraderie" was set up to try to abandon their duty and escape. Some have paid with their life for the evasion, many, indeed, of the hidden collaborators and soldiers at the German landing (the number of evasions is estimated to be around 800) could be repaired in Turkey, aided by undercover organization or by the Catholic Mission and Italians, all united in the same feeling of love for their homeland but hate for fascism and anti Germans attitude. [...]

Of great importance is the attitude of the Carabinieri who, for several months, refused the German military oath, merely accepting the one required of civil servants. They always favoured the many soldiers with the release of identity documents to avoid the capture. On several occasions their behaviour was superior to any expectation, such as when, from December 28, 1943 to January 1, 1944, they resisted the German imposition of execution by hanging two death sentences of saboteurs pronounced by the German court.

The same refusal they posed when, in mid-March 1945 (despite the armed threat of a German company under the command of the infamous Keller who *turned his arms against 17 helpless Carabinieri), the execution of the death sentence be carried out by hanging, of 6 civilians convicted by the Military Tribunal for collaboration with the Allies.*

Recalling, we also like to point out the attitude of challenge taken in November 1943 by the commander of the Carabinieri towards centurion Tetro Michele, who, with his CC.NN. ("Black shirts") tended to replace the Carabinieri police tasks because they were obstacles for their bully activities.

Escape and desertion were not prerogatives of the Italian military. A British Intelligence report informed that General Weichs warned his soldiers of the dangers they would face if they had attempted desertion.

British Intelligence Report No 3078
Kalimnos - Greece
Dodecanese: Naval / Military
Kalymnos
D. ....
E. Commander in Chief, General Weichs, in order to prevent desertions from Calimno, informs that Turkish "Black Cats" patrol those waters searching for German deserters, killing them after terrible torture against all international law. No German had escaped such a fate; therefore those soldiers who wanted to desert are aware of what they would encounter.
F. ....

Escape after the capture

The escape of Italian soldiers was often facilitated by Greek fishermen and owners of boats who, without caring for the danger and trusting in good fortune, were transporting the fugitives to the nearby islands where they were then picked up by British personnel and transferred to special camps. Others, however, relying on their energy, swam across that stretch of sea often beaten by strong winds; others still had to decide if, once in the sea, it was worth trying the crossing to avoid capture.

Captain Squeo recounts his difficult experiences since he was captured on the 4th of October near the isthmus and was transferred to Cos Castle along with Lieutenant Aiello and other officers.

(Squeo)[...] *On the evening of October 12, following a clear refusal given to the centurion Tetro of the former Fascist Militia who proposed to redeem us by adhering to the Germans troops, we sailed with another 700 Italian prisoners on the Greek steamboat "Santorini" to Piraeus and, thereafter, to Germany.*

We were ordered to go down into the ship's hold through the only vertical ladder in the hatchway. There was a real cluster of humanity. We were unbelievably crammed. I removed my shoes, took off my pants and jacket, and counting on my good swimming ability I began to plan the escape.

About an hour after our departure from the harbour, around 1900, allied planes gunned and bombarded the ship repeatedly until a huge shock made us realize that the steamboat had been hit.

Despite the confusion that had been created, I managed to reach the deck. A rocket launched by planes illuminated the scene like daytime. The Germans fired on us to silence the panic and threw hand grenades into the holds to prevent other prisoners from coming up to the deck. I took advantage of the confusion, crossed the parapet and dived into the water. Others imitated my gesture. I avoided the turbulance produced by the propellers.

The Germans were machine gunning us from the ship. Aware of the sad end I would have if caught, after a quick orientation I got better, I swam in the direction of Turkey.

Many died in the water, struck by machine guns and many because they were swallowed by the waves, including Captain Simeone, Sergeant Major Zaccaria and others.

I swam all night. After 11 hours of swimming and suffering, I finally reached the Anatolian coast at Kefaluka where, more dead than alive, I was picked up by two Turkish fishermen living on the coast.

They made the women move away from the cottage because I was completely naked and took me into the house. They placed me on the ground and offered hot water drinks as refreshment. On the same morning two Turkish soldiers accompanied me to the police station where I met Captain Pietro Sozzi, Lieutenant Rendine and another 30 soldiers from my same steamer who reached the shore using wreckage [...] In the same afternoon we were led to Bodrum where we declared to the authority of the place that we were all Badoglio soldiers.

Each of us had to give a report on the recent facts. Turkish citizens offered us for piety some worn clothing. A few days later we were taken to the Tefenni camp where badoglians were gathered; fascist, instead, were concentrated in a camp near Ankara.

Little assisted and rather poorly treated by the Turks, we stayed until February 27, 1944 when, following the intervention of the Italian Embassy in Turkey, the Anglo-American authorities investigated our full adherence to the decision to continue fighting the Germans, we were taken to Syria and then to an allied camp in El Gaza, Palestine. We stayed for more than a month then went to Suez for boarding.

On May 4, 1944, we landed at Taranto and gathered at the Corigliano reorganizational camp in the province of Lecce.

After five years of overseas military service I was put on leave. I finally met my loved ones who since the 10th February 1944 were informed of my death by shooting.

Lieutenant Aiello was unable to follow Captain Squeo. He was wounded on one arm and remained on the ship. Then he returned to the port at Cos and was hospitalized at Hippocrateous Hospital. Aiello confirms that the Germans fired on the shipwrecks to prevent Italians soldiers from escaping to Turkey.

The relations between German troops and Italian adherents were never friendly and worsened with the events despite the complete adherence to Captain Nasca's German cause.

The continued desertion of fighters and workers was a clear proof of the feelings of our soldiers and at the beginning of '45 the German Command adopted concentration measures to all workers and soldiers in Antimachia. In the following April all Italian soldiers were disarmed.

Another officer, Captain Orlando, reports that:

"[...] I was hospitalized at Coo, with the help of a sailor I managed to escape with other officers. In the village of Bodrum I met with an English officer who asked me if I was willing to go to the Army that Marshal Badoglio was forming in Italy. I agreed, though, the wound on my arm had produced an anchilosis due to a nerve injury. In an English hospital, in Cyprus, I received treatment then I was sent to Al Qantarah where I stayed until September 9, 1944. I was enrolled in an Italian pioneer collaborators company in Kassassin, Egypt, and on July 31, 1945, I was discharged for disability. "

SPASMODIC SEARCH OF RELATIVE'S NEWS

On December 10, 1945, Margherita sent a letter to the Albo d'Oro [26] following a request to the Ministry of War on November 27, 1944, saying: *I am doctor Antonio Anselmi's wife begging you to read and deepen the investigation to find seriously reliable and concrete elements on what happened to him. Father Bacheca of the Cos Parish, in response to my postcard, announced that my husband, on October 3, 1943, fell prisoner of the Germans after having performed nobly his duty and that between 5 and 8 of the same month disappeared; some time later, in late March, his suspected end was ascertained considering he was part of the large group of Italian Officers - perhaps over one hundred - who fell victim to German fury.*

He says that his wedding ring and a cigarette case that could be attributed to him by the inscription of two interlaced As (Antonio Anselmi) had been recovered during the excavations; that a bank colleague of him confirmed its ownership while others could not make similar statements and that there was at least one other officer, Arminio Antonio, Sicilian, with the same initials.

It also appears to me that Albo d'Oro had received from the same source, shortly before, a list of the Cos killed officers, including 66 recovered bodies and among them there was an Anselmi Antonio (?!)

So, who are these wretched men? Military or civilians? Moreover, with regard to my husband, where did this statement reporting only his name and surname come from?

In the report, even if compiled by a special commission, it could and should result much more detail because my husband had to have his own identification tag and other personal cards, even if soaked or deteriorated ones, from which it could have been possible to find the paternity, the birth date, the matriculation number and the recruiting centre, etc. ... and even when there were nothing – it seems difficult to think - in the extreme, it would always have been right to give an opinion about the dental shape, certainly existing, with the number and place of any fillings (in gold or

---

[26] Albo d'Oro = Gold Board of the Fallen in War

otherwise) in order to be as precise as possible and to make it likely, at first glance, to have some idea of whether or not it could be my husband knowing quite well the number of fillings. If nothing of the human remains and clothing could be obtained, how can one say that the body belonged to Anselmi Antonio? The coincidences are so weird to make possible mistakes to similiarities.

Father Bacheca, in his clearest good faith, relies upon the sad news on two points: the end of Anselmi Antonio has been established and his bridal ring and a cigarette holder recovered. However he does not say how that sad ending has been established. So for the ring and for the cigarette case he does not say in what way they have been recovered, that is, whether it is on the body or elsewhere, while raising the doubt that another Sicilian officer, Arminio Antonio, had the same destiny...

This letter highlights all the anguish of those who await the return of a relative. But it was not the only one. Mrs. Elisa, who lost at Cos her husband and her son-in-law, both of them Army Officers, concludes her short and sorrowful letter with these words: *After an anxiety that lasts for 31 months, we wait for reliable news that will comfort us or cause us to fall into the greatest and irreparable pain. May the sacrifice of our loved ones be helpful to rebuild our poor, tormented Country.*

There was fear to cast doubt on the work done with great care by a group of people, including a medical doctor, who had to examine the bodies of 66 men buried for one year in a terribly marshy soil. Father Bacheca, in addition, besides writing on the above mentioned reports, did a hard job in answering all the letters of the relatives asking for news. In 37, however, they did not have any response since their end were never defined.

The Municipalities' Offices of a single Officer's origin, the parishes asked for interceding throughout the Vatican, the Ministry of War, the Italian Red Cross and the International Comité of Croix Rouge, the Commission for the Protection of the Italian's interests in the Dodecanese, the Cos parish priest, officers and military personnel of all ranks returned from the island or from prison camps in Germany have been questioned by the desperate relatives for the missing family members.

The informative procedure triggered off by the Italian Red Cross – Prisoners' Bureau - who reported the death of military personnel to the Ministry of War and the latter informed the Municipalities in order to pass the news on to the families *"with all due precaution for the case ..."* specifying that *"our communication is purely informative because the official one will be transmitted by the competent Ministry ... "*. In fact, the ministerial commission in March 1947 in one of the many cases wrote: *examined the Lieutenant Aiello Enzo report No. 4368 /I on 17/9/45.... and following the Italian Red Cross note No. A.815358 of April 9, 1946, confirms the death of the Officer on October 3, 1943, stating that "nothing comes from the existing documents, but, given the circumstances in which the death occurred, it is considers that the act of death was not compiled at the time and, as far as possible, it is proposed the relevant declaration."*

The judgment was then validated by the Inter-ministerial Commission.

However, some families were not satisfied with such a communication. There are those who have spent all the years, from that fateful 1943, waiting for their husband, son or brother next to a window with their gaze lost in the void and sketching a slight, outspoken smile every time they saw a person advancing in the street.

A young lady waited eight years before she married. She had asked for news of the loved one all the offices, to those who, to her knowledge, had been on that island. She had to surrender to the evidence. She married and had children, perhaps, without ever forgetting that young 21 year old handsome man who she fell in love with. Then, when she was a widow, she knew of a meeting in Assisi of Lasalliani, students of the Christian schools in Rhodes, and had the will to make proper inquires. She was told of a lady in Cos, Eleni Klonari; she got in touch with her and was given a name of a person in Italy who, for some years, had been studying the case. She then knew, after almost 65 years, what had happened to her young lover officer; he was one of the 37, out of 103, ever sought after.

Mrs. Carola, in one of her afflicted letters, appealed to the Ministry to "*ask the Allied Government for permission to send a mission (possibly made up of some family members of the Fallen) to Cos as already required by Father Ferdinando Meconi - chaplain of the 10th Infantry Regiment. That the Government should make provision for other excavations since, according to Father Sportoletti, another chaplain of the same regiment still in Cos, other graves should be in Lambi and in St. John. That the Ministry requested Father Michelangelo Bacheca, Cos parish, who attended at the exhumation of the victims, saw all the objects and documents found and provided a detailed report; that an inquiry for investigations be opened.*"

Captain Nasca, on July 29, 1944, responded from Cos to Matilde Gay, a girlfriend of an Officer, who had requested information about him by letter of May 30 of the same year: "*I've known and remember your fiancé who was an aide in the sector where I commanded an antiaircraft battery and I remember very well that he was the highest of all. I will describe in summary the facts that took place on the island after the disgraceful and unfortunate 8 September. Accepted as friendly by a group of irresponsible and indecisive officers, on 13 September landed on the island some English gentlemen posing as masters and protectors. A well-organized propaganda convinced several commanders that they had to fight the Germans, and all of them, with poor foresight persisted in persuading the mass of soldiers who were to serve as cannon fodder.*

On October 3, the Germans landed on the island and, while the British were trying to escape, they ordered our infantry to attack. The giant stampede was successful, and the Germans occupied the island in 30 hours. The only Unit that remained compact and always alongside the German comrades was that of the undersigned. Regarding your fiancé I can tell you that after the occupation he left with all the other officers for Greece to be imprisoned in Germany. I cannot say anything to you and I am astonished as he has not written to you yet.

It would be enough to read these words to get the idea of Captain Nasca. It's worth adding few lines: *I hope, in a few days to gather more news among the soldiers. It will be my duty to inform you. I thank you for the expressed wishes you have made for me. May the Lord fulfill all our prayers for the salvation of our country, our honour, and our families.*

The fact that he is alive already means so much to you. Your letter is the first I received from Italy. You cannot imagine what and how emotional I have been.

Another pearl of courage and honesty is offered by 2nd Lieutenant Pierrajmond who writes to the Poggiani family on 2 January XXII (1944) [27]: *He was my great companion during his stay on Cos. Your son was on a coastal battery a short distance (about 1km and 1/2) from that which was for many months my command. I have been in his company many times; we were great comrades. I saw him last time on September 26 last; he was in good physical condition, only worried about the lack of news. We talked about our experiences in Croatia and of my own in Albania. We had spent many hours together before we departed. At that time on our island there were British troops landed there after the shameful armistice.*

On October 3 at 6 am, German troops began attacking the island and took it in less than 24 hours. German parachutists rained right on the 136 battery that was the first to surrender after firing against them. The captain in command was captured, however, knowing the German language, he was employed to convey the German order to surrender to other Italian Units.

I knew this from Captain Squeo, his commander. I did not see him and I

---

[27] XXII : it means 22nd year of the Fascist era

think he is in some place in Greece or the Balkan states interned by German troops. Instead, I put myself with my soldiers at the disposal of the Reich and with them I stayed until November 28, 1943, XXII, when I was sent on leave. This is all I can say with the fervent wish that the victory of the German and Republican Fascist troops will bring you back your son. Fascist greetings.

If the captain and his subordinate had said the truth to the families they would have avoided suffering and living in anxiety of a likely return.

The correspondence of the Poggiani family continued over the time and the following is a communication published on "Il Piccolo di Trieste" on January 18, 1944.

COMUNICATI

Dal giorno 8 settembre s. a. non si hanno notizie del S. ten. PIERINO POGGIANI, 55 Regg. da posizione, 136.a Batt., P. M. 550 (Isola di Coo). Chiunque ne avesse notizia è pregato di comunicarla alla famiglia Luigi Poggiani in Cervignano del Friuli.

A note on Captain Nasca

Colonel Mondini was responsible for the Historic Office of the Army General Staff. One of his tasks was collecting reports of military personnel returning home from prison camps and civilians expelled from the Dodecanese Islands. In the letter sent to the Secretariat Office, he wrote as follows about Captain Camillo Nasca:

The main guilty officer appears to be the Artillery Captain Camillo Nasca, commander of the 62ⁿᵈ battery, who on October 3, 1943, as the Germans just started disembarking operations instead of shooting with his battery against enemy troops, with a real act of betrayal, immediately changed to their side and opened fire against the positions held by the Italian-British. Not enough. He wanted to be a propagandist in favour of the Germans and did not refrain from pursuing those Italian compatriots who refused to adhere to his ideas.

Even more repugnant was his attitude towards the respect of the shot Italian officers: he never cared about them and was against the exhumation so that it was necessary to take advantage of his absence to obtain authorization from the German authorities to proceed with the research of the graves. For these reasons it is believed that Nasca must be denounced to the Martial Court.

With Captain Nasca is also liable for denouncing Lieutenant Pierraymond, his subordinate, who, at the refusal to open fire by the soldiers personally himself fired against the Italian-British positions.

For this reason, after the war, when he returned to Italy, he was denounced and, despite his long defensive memory, condemned to prison.

On the left, sitting, Captain Nasca. Standing, behind the German, 2ⁿᵈ Lieut Pierrajmond

135

THE UNCERTAIN FATE OF THE
103 OFFICERS AFTER THEIR CAPTURE

Father Bacheca writes in one of his reports that there were 148 Italian officers in service at Cos on October 3, 1943. Of these 7 collaborated with Germans, 10 hospitalized and then transferred to Germany, the remaining 131 were subjected to a farcical process. 28 were excused of the accusation of having taken part in the fighting because they were Medical Officers, Chaplains, and Service Officers; some of them managed to escape to Turkey. The 103 were found guilty and shortly afterward they began "departing" in small groups towards the port of Tingachi. Perhaps they thought they were being taken to prison camps in Germany, and instead, near a grove, a machine-gunner, hiding in a bush, cut them down.

Who were those 103 men? Most of them, 84, were just over twenty. The older lieutenant reached 28 years of age. They were mostly graduate or graduate students with a bag of nationalism incited them by fascist propaganda; all registered at the GUF - Young University Fascists. An example of their belief is offered by 2nd Lieutenant Michele D'Amore, commander of the Linopoti machine gun platoon, quoted by soldier De Prosperis in his informative report. In one of his letter to his beloved, on April 16, 1943, he wrote:

O.Z. 16 April, 1943- XXI

Let fade away the pains. Let increase the virtues of our people in these days of heroic resistance in the Italian fighting in the sunny Tunisia. The great certainty of victory let not diminish and more and more be rooted in the inhuman massacres that highly civilized people do on our enviable beautiful Italian cities.

The spirit of every Italian soldier, day by day, gets hardened and finds new energy for the hard war. Everywhere and always the daring ardor is craved by our fighter. Again, here the hearts pulsate for the war that physically is fought elsewhere but in each of us burn with anger against the tractable enemy that never gives us the open satisfaction of showing itself to the continuous hard proof we all seek here.

The consciousness does not mind the sad consequences of reality, but it is mercilessly human to the supreme misfortunes of friends who were with you yesterday, confident of young ideals and of the great hopes to come, and today immolate for the defence and greatness of Homeland with dread of useless life for those who do not use it for God, Homeland and Family.

Great companions are really those who, by example, demonstrate to others the fatal path to the attainment of the great ideality that all our people have prefixed with the irrevocable will to realize it with the sure victory for us. It is a must to imitate them to be worthy of their friendship.

In the period from April 16 to August 23, 1943, Michele used to refer to the certain victory, the triumph of the just, the defeat of the barbarians notwithstanding the happenings around the world.

Since the autumn of '42, when Michele was travelling to reach his overseas location, the course of II GM was in favour of the Allies: on 4 November the Italian-Germans suffered the defeat in the battle of El Alamein and, in the following 8, US General Eisenhower's Troops landed in Morocco and Algeria. Despite the defeat of Stalingrad, Hitler decided to strengthen the units in Africa to oppose the enemy troops. It was an unnecessary effort, Italian and German forces capitulated on the other side of the Mediterranean in May 1943.

The loss of Libya and the maritime "Mare Nostrum" dominion other than the heavy catastrophe suffered by the ARMIR [28] in Russia weakened the fascist regime trust in the Country and the political

---

[28] ARMIR: three divisions, called the Italian Expedition Corps in Russia (CSIR), went to the eastern front in mid-July 1941. Initially framed in the 11th German Army and then in Panzergruppe 1. CSIR participated in the campaign until April 1942 when the requirements of the battle front demanded two other Italian armies that together with the CSIR were brought together in the 8th Army or Armada Italiana in Russia (ARMIR). Located south of the River Don, the 8th Army, together with the 2nd Hungarian Army and the 3rd Romanian Army, should have covered the left flank of the German forces that were advancing to Stalingrad at that time.

position of Mussolini became increasingly precarious so that, immediately after the landing of the Allies in Sicily on July 10, 1943 with the Husky operation, he was removed from his office.

King Vittorio Emanuele III directed Marshal Pietro Badoglio to rule the nation with the intention of bringing Italy out of the conflict. On September 8, an armistice was concluded with the Anglo Americans, and on that occasion the King moved, at night and in secret, to Brindisi with his court and representatives of the government headed by Badoglio, leaving Italy at the mercy of German repression that did not wait. The nation was divided into two, Monarchy, centre-south of Italy and Republic in the north; Partisan forces opposed the German-fascist units in the central-northern region, the civil war was now afflicting the nation. It was a period of great suffering for the reaction of Germany and for the bombings of the new Allies onto the North of Italy who thwarted Hitler's resistance.

So how does Michele and the other 102 officers refuse to cooperate with the German armed forces still allied to the Mussolini government set up in Salò? They kept faith in the oath to the King although he left Italy in disarray. The words they uttered then returned to their mind when asked the question.

"I swear to be faithful to His Majesty the King and His Real Successors, to respectfully observe the Statute and other laws of the State and to fulfill all the duties of my State with the sole purpose of the inseparable good of the King and of the Fatherland"

To this oath was added an edict of the King emanating from his new residence to all the units: no one can remove the military from the commitment of loyalty. That was how they faced their destiny with courage.

2nd Lieut D'Amore letter to Maria: front and back
A note written by Maria on the top right:
"War is approaching, its consequences"

139

THE RESPONSIBILITIES

The Responsibilities

Responsibility for Linopoti has to be directed upon General Wilhelm Friedrich Müller, Commander of the 22nd German Infantry Division, who carried out the invasion of Cos on October 3, 1943 and later on the nearby island of Leros. The crimes that stained him are far beyond those of the 103 Italian officers. Civilian and military "badogliani" were subjected to a long period of terror and many perished due to his anger.

No less cruel and responsible were, however, the subordinate commanders for the barbarous way with which they proceeded to massacre.

Who, on the other hand, have moral responsibilities?

These are to be attributed to those who, despite knowing Italian military unpreparedness, have made the people part of an extended war in time and space; who has run a long and indefinite negotiation to reach the Anglo – American armistice and for the late declaration of war to support Germany; who has caused the ineffective British intervention in the Dodecanese, and, finally, the Italian politics concealing criminal war records failing to reward justice to the memory of the Fallen.

General Friedrich Wilhelm Müller

General Müller was the CO of the 22nd German Division based in Crete. He received the order to attack and conquer Cos and then Leros.

At the end of the Cos operation he informed his superior command in Athens he had carried out his task, got possession of a lot of enemy armament, material and fuel, captured 900 British and 3,000 Italian soldiers and executed 89 Italian Army Officers.

General Müller did have an important role in the massacre; being the Commander he was the main person responsible.

Almost a year later, in 1944, he surrendered with his unit in Yugoslavia. Once captured, he was consigned to the Greek authorities and in 1947 he was charged with 7 capital crimes involving the death of civilians and sentenced to 20 years imprisonment also being responsible for the destruction of villages by fire. In 1947 he was sentenced and executed on the date of the German Crete invasion.

The sentence referred only to charges committed in Greece against the Greek population. For crimes committed in Greece against civilian and Italian military personnel, Italian Justice should have dealt with him. It never happened.

It was pure coincidence that the Cos massacre came to light. It was due to a letter dated 26 January 1946 sent to the Italian War Minister written 27 months after the events on Cos, by the father in law of an Italian officer, Lieutenant Antonio Anselmi, serving on Cos in 1943.

Left : General Müller surrounded by Greek Officers on the day of the trial
Right: Gen Müller, Capt Kullman and Italian Officer prisoners

He wanted information about his relative [29]. The minister sent the petition to the relevant Allied Office in London requiring the

---

[29] The incipit of the letter: *A great and terrible crime that cries revenge in the sight of God is the one fullfilled by General Franz Ferdinando Müller, the bewildering thirsty beast for human blood who, based on the fantastic reasons for war, had premeditated, arranged and on his own accord that horrible excide, should not have more peace on this land because innumerable infernal tongues of fire coming from his victims and relatives will converge on him pointing to his disgraced conscience; nor will it be possible to justify himself one day at the rendering of the accounts, and even less appeal to the Supreme Judgment of Eternal Life.*

extradition of General Müller for prosecution. Sometime later, German Authorities replied that no General Müller existed in that country. The reason being the Christian name was wrong; his name was Wilhelm Friedrich and not Franz Ferdinand.

For this reason, the Fallen of Cos and their families had no justice at all. Maria, the wife of Lieutenant Gaspare Nocera was twenty years of age and the mother of one baby at the time her husband was killed. She must thank Greek Justice for calling General Müller to account.

The Dux, Benito Mussolini

In order to get a seat at the "Table of The Great of The world" Mussolini took a great gamble when he boasted of the power of Italian armed Forces.

Mussolini was an example of the worst kind of braggart, boasting that his Air Force was capable of spraying London with poisoned gas, when, actually, none of his aircraft were suitable for air combat.

He also lied about the strength of the Italian Army, by doing some "creative accountancy" with how the regiments and battalions were composed. He said he could call upon 73 Infantry Divisions {24 were fully efficient, 29 not completed, 20 scarcely efficient} and 2 Armoured Divisions having inadequate tanks and motor vehicles for a long battle.

He had just increased artificially the number of the available Units; he took one regiment from a division and a battalion from a regiment and so on. The units subtracted formed other battalions, regiments and divisions.

The Navy was without radar; although studies were conducted in Italy and the projects, having reached the final phase, were ready to be actuated.

Logistics: Italy had fuel, ammunition, spare parts for only few months of supply and the worst is that she depended on other countries for supply of the important items.

Armaments were obsolete residues of World War 1

He had looked enviously at how Hitler's Forces had stormed through Europe using Blitzkrieg tactics, and he thought his Forces could emulate them. It was unfortunate that at that time, he was surrounded by sycophant Senior Officers who were all "Yes man", none of whom had the courage or indeed the inclination to challenge his quixotic schemes.

In the Dodecanese, his forces were badly motivated and homesick, some of them never having been home for up to 7 years. They were equipped with obsolete weapons and the lack of supplies, especially personal items, increasing their disenchantment and demoralization.

There was a song in those years of war; it said:

Colonel, I do not want water,
Give me the destroying fire
Since the blood of my heart
Will extinguish my thirst.

Certainly if those boys had improved equipment and welfare, they would have given a better account of themselves in the battles to come.

Marshall Pietro Badoglio

After Mussolini, the person who must bear a large measure of responsibility for the Italian disaster is General Badoglio. For two years before the fall of Mussolini (25th July 1943) he was the Chief of General War Staff and after that date he was elected Prime Minister with the primary task of negotiating an Armistice, getting Italy out of The War and changing to The Allied side.

Before September 1943 he personally tried to arrive at an Armistice with the Allies so he already knew when he became Prime Minster the conditions for it. He wasted time; he wanted to obtain advantage knowing he was not in a position to ask but to accept. His main aim was to save the King and his family and himself. He was so frightened of the German reaction that he waited for events to happen. 38 days past before finalizing an armistice. It was during these days of indecision and delay that German troops occupied important, strategic sites in Italy, transferring 18 divisions.

He waited 35 days after the armistice was announced before declaring war on Germany (13 October 1943). This is why the Italians on the whole were considered traitors. But the soldiers did respect their oath to the king who had left the country to avoid the vengeance of the Nazis. The majority of the soldiers, sailors and airmen did their utmost to honour their responsibility to their flag.

Mr. Winston Churchill and his intervention in the Dodecanese

Churchill must bear some responsibility for the tragedy because of his lack of foresight in evaluating the true realities of the military situation in the Dodecanese. One of his main aims was to disrupt the activities of the Luftwaffe in the central Mediterranean. He also failed to realize that the islands of the Dodecanese were mostly occupied by the German troops, with the exception of Cos, Leros and Symi.

His main faults, as a personal point of view, were irresolution due to his incapability of facing the enemy and his inconsideration for the great number of victims and loss of materiel.

In his book, "Churchill's Folly" Antony Rogers said that Churchill' intervention in the Aegean was his last defeat, after that there were only victories.

This might be true, but defeat on Cos could have been avoided. Perhaps if he had waited a few months the course of the events would have been different. Anyway, it is known, History does not base itself upon "ifs".

The Files Cover up

This aspect is not directly related to the battle of Cos but to the tragedy that took place afterward. For years the Italian public was unaware of what happened to their countrymen on that island, indeed, even today, very little is known about the historical facts.

In the late 1940's and 50's the Allies saw Federal West Germany as a buffer State against the threat posed by Soviet Russia. As a consequence of this, "a blind eye" was turned to the composition of the new German Army, which contained many officers and NCO's who had served in the Wehrmacht in WW2. Some of these men had been involved in war crimes.

To make things even more difficult, the Allies declared a "Statute of Limitations" on the prosecution of war criminals, effectively allowing 100's if not 1,000's to escape Justice.

Italy followed suit, but what was kept very secret was the existence of a filing cabinet filled with the details of war crimes and war criminals . The files of many crimes that occurred in Italy and abroad against the Italians were closed in a bookcase placed in a closet out of sight. It contained 695 files of which 415 were complete names of the persons committing the crimes. Besides a register was found; it listed 2,000 crimes listing names, places, penal code number to which the crime was referring to, and some more details.

Those crimes referred to 1943, '44 and '45; they were sent finally to Prosecutors in the years 1994, '95 and '96. Exactly 50 years later.

Only one process reached sentence; it was that of Captain Erich Priebke, who was accused of participating in the mass executions at the Ardeatine Caves where 330 Italians were shot in retaliation for the death of 33 German soldiers, killed by partisans in via Rasella, a street in Rome.

One day, in 1994, a person who remains unknown sent a document to Franco Giustolisi, a journalist, who did the investigation. The filing cabinet was found and it was given the name: "The Shameful Filing Cabinet" [30].

---

[30] "An old, ministerial, dark-browned cabinet tarled in several parts. It was at the end of a dirty corridor of the Military General Attorney in Rome.

THE REGIMENT'S FLAG

Saving the regiment's flag was the concern of many Italians on the island and relatively much effort by the Germans that for months had been busy looking for it. They found the flag sheath devoid of its content and its decorations.

Sister Clotilde Santini [31] reported in her diary, November 10, 1943, that Germans were still in search of the flag and the regiment's safe; they thought it might have been hidden in their convent.

Who physically saved the emblem?

Giuseppe Esposito, the switchboard operator at Prophet Elias, in his report writes:

«I found the glorious flag and its sheath. The emblem with its six medals were at first hidden by me under the soil in the hospital garden next to the fence and then, closed in a tin canister, I transferred the lot to a safer place. I went to Caginicolau Stergo family in Asfendiu village; I knew them since 1939. I told the head of the house the vicissitude of the flag and after receiving an oath to not proffer any word about it to anyone, we buried it in the garden of the family's home after having enclosed it in a terracotta pot and, then, in a tin to preserve it from moisture.

A few days before my departure, I confided the secret to a primary Italian teacher, Coridali Flora from Conselice. She would replace me in the risky assignment in the event of my misfortune. I did not know who the flag was delivered to at the time of Cos liberation. The reason being I was taken by the Germans to a prison camp since September 1944.»

«The sergeant was afraid he could be suddenly taken away not having the possibility to carry safely those objects with him» confirmed Miss Coridali in her report. She continued saying: «He had already found the person to leave the flag with. I was disappointed with the decision since I could have kept it safe. However, I promised and I kept my secret until May 9, 1945. When the war ended, imagining the British landing on the islands would act as new owners, I thought it was necessary to pass the heavy burden to Dante

---

[31] A nurse nun at the Hippocrateous Hospital

Zucchelli, Lieutenant of Carabinieri, who I was in a friendly relationship with. I was afraid of the Greek family blackmailing. Zucchelli promised me to solve the delicate matter. I begged him to do everything possible to solve the case and he promised me: "I will do whatever is possible to solve the very delicate question"»

Miss Coridali returned to Italy as a Red Cross nurse to accompany forced repatriating Italian families from the Aegean islands and had no news of the flag except when summoned to the Ministry of War to deliver her report on the period spent in Cos. Only then she learnt the flag had been recovered by Lieutenant Zucchelli and that it was safe in Rhodes.

The inquiries carried out by the officer were indeed very scrupulous and he describes the events in two of his reports: «*The vicissitudes of that precious symbol, loaded with ancient traditions.*»

"Following the German occupation, anxiety about the fate of the regimental flag remained in the minds of Italians officers, soldiers and civilians. No news about it» Zucchelli reported. «*At the time of the German landing, the flag was hidden in an artificial cavity of a small house roof beam up at Prophet Elia hill where the Regiment Tactical Command was located. Lieutenant Salvatore Coratza was the ensign bearer thus responsible for its custody. It was generally thought the officer managed to circumvent the Germans' vigilance and fled to Anatolia. So, among the remaining officers, the hope was he could have carried the flag with him».*

Meanwhile, the Germans had found the empty sheath and continued to search for the emblem. To this end, by mid-October, Major Saldern, deputy commander of the German assault group, and Lieutenant Vogel, Orstkommandant of the city, questioned the Italian officers hospitalized at Hippocrateus Hospital, the last survivors on the island.

Among all, captains Floccia, regimental aide, and Orlando, the garrison's command aide, plus Lieutenant Zucchelli himself, underwent continuous, pressing and tight interrogations.

It was useless. Even considering they would have released such information, they were not aware where the flag could be. Some days later, the first two officers escaped from the hospital and reached Turkey. Zucchelli, remained on the island, pledging to discover the flag before the Germans.

There were two possibilities at that moment: the flag could be in Italian hands or delivered by an Italian citizen to a Greek person for temporary custody. In both cases it was advisable to act circumspectly avoiding any suspicion.

Zucchelli shared his ideas with Gianazzi, a Navy Lieutenant. They agreed on the future efforts aiming at the recovery.

After a few months, the Germans abandoned the search as well as some other Italian civilians did. By then, no one but the two officers, was interested in that particular search.

Logic pushed Lieutenant Zucchelli to turn his attention to the latest military presence in the place where the flag possibly had been hidden. Among them suspicion fell on a Giuseppe Esposito who was known to have been the last leaving the stronghold. The hypothesis was corroborated by the news of some civilians who had pervaded in vain the premises where the flag could be found before the Germans entered. The officer established careful vigilance around sergeant Esposito and his young Greek girlfriend who visited him frequently at the Linopoti Hospital.

Following the transfer of Esposito to a prison camp in Macedonia, the lieutenant's attentions turned to the girl and her family, especially after receiving the confession of Miss Coridali, the teacher.

Zucchelli and Gianazzi decided to act cautiously and wait for better times while keeping watch over the young woman and her family.

But, « at the first appearance of allied troops » wrote Lieutenant Zucchelli, «the Greek population demonstrated, with morbid exaltation excesses their phobia for everything that had an Italian origin ».

People and things were united in the insane, absurd mania in every possible way. The custodian of the flag was unfortunately amongst the most inflamed families who considered it a privilege to belong to Asfendiù village, the most turbulent and the vocal anti-Italian demonstrators in the Dodecanese.

In fact, Ciriaca Caginicolau's feelings soon appeared clear: Esposito was just the past. Nonetheless, in late 1945, on his return to Italy from a prison camp, he tried to re-establish the interrupted union with his girlfriend. He did not know how significantly the Greek-Italian relations had changed in the meantime. As Zucchelli wrote: « *racial hatred had overtaken affection, while her family were among the representatives of the island advocating publicly the need, generally proclaimed, to break every link with Italy and the Italians* ».

Fortunately the sequel came with the intervention of the British police Cos commander, Captain Lennard, arrived on the island after the surrender of the Germans and became Zucchelli and Gianazzi's friend.

By making authoritarian and threatening heavy sanctions, Lennard forced the Caginicolau family to deliver the emblem.

At first they denied, but one day Father Caginicolau went to Lieutenant Zucchelli to intervene in favour of the two sons who had been found in possession of weapons and therefore imprisoned. This facilitated the conclusion of the story.

The flag was finally returned, though in misery, with four of its six gold medals. Zucchelli knew that one medal was lost and another was in Coridali's hands given to her by Esposito to prove he had the flag.

Lieutenant Zucchelli criticized Esposito. He wrote: « *he entrusted the flag of his regiment and of so many other martyrs to a local family instead of any of the Italians who remained on Cos with infinite possibilities to preserve it equally safely as the Caginicolau and with more infinite care and love. Esposito must have reflected on such thoughts before being taken prisoner if he felt the need to confide with Miss Coridali* ».

She, however, despite promising absolute secrecy, in the face of her own conscience, could not withstand the need to confide in someone who was more suitable to be part of such a secret.

Her gesture is all the more meritorious since she had close friendships with the Germans, from whose side she had fled to the point of asking, when Cos was freed by the British, to follow them as a Red Cross nurse. Her loyalty came to request the Italian officer to promise all his interest in the recovery of the flag and not leave it in Greek hands. She recommended all the merit of the flag's salvation fell on Esposito himself.

Zucchelli concludes: «... *in order to avoid the flag running the risk of my eventual personal misfortune, in December 1945 I handed it to the "Commission for the Protection of the Italians' Interest in the Dodecanese," The flag joined others saved by love of the Italians in the Aegean.* »

Today the flag with its medals is preserved in the Vittoriano Museum in Rome at the Altar of the Country. It was delivered by Friar Felice Vincenti, of the Franciscan Mission of Rhodes, awarded "Knight of Merit of the Order of the Italian Republic" (27 December 1975) and "Officer of Merit of the Order of the Italian Republic" (2 October 1995).

Colonel Luigi Mondini, in those days Chief of the Army Staff History Archives, collected all reports released by the personnel returning from abroad after the war. He proposed decorations to a certain number of Army personnel, soldiers and officers. Sergeant Major Giuseppe Esposito was one of them. His commitment in saving the flag was completely ignored.

THE MEMORIES OF A MACHINE GUNNER

Severino De Prosperis left Barletta (Apulia) on October 7, 1942. He was twenty years old. His destination was the Dodecanese which he knew only from what he learned at school. He reached Mestre (outskirt of Venice) with a train made up of cattle wagons and then to Piraeus in a third-class carriage. He crossed the Balkan region in a gruelling and dangerous journey due to partisan assaults; the journey was made in sixteen endless days. He remained 45 days along with many other compatriots, waiting for their destination to be reached, in a camp near the Athens airport. Finally, on December 8, he sailed for Rhodes with the steamer Villa Argentina and then, with the Bucintoro Navy ship, arrived in Kos. Navigation lasted for three days.

The journey was exhausting, the waiting awful, unimaginable hygiene. Then the quarantine with his travelling companions. He was welcomed by a healthy shower; his garments were boiled to remove the colonies of lice that infested them. It was there that he experienced his first misadventure: some old soldiers tried, although without success, to pinch his shoes. They needed them because they were wearing wooden clogs as the ships with supplies awaited from Italy were late to arrive or even were intercepted and sunk by the British Navy.

Severino was assigned to a machine gun squad in service at Kefalos, at the west end of the island, and then to Prophet Elijah, a hill located halfway to the capital where his platoon was garrisoned Alikes Tipakiou. The location was upstream of the only island's longitudinal road of Cos – Kefalo, located near a pond and a stone house for the armoury, the ammunition depot and the military lodging: in the lower floor platoon's commander, 2nd Lieutenant Michele D'Amore, and in the upper floor the machine gunners.

The surrounding area was scarcely inhabited and the soldiers did not have transport vehicles to reach the town. On Sundays a military truck was available for the personnel, free from service, to spend some time in town. Severino took advantage of it to go to the mass in the "Regina" Barracks and stay some time among the islanders who spoke his language.

He was on guard in the night 2 to 3 October 1943. At about 0700 he came into action against a German motorbike patrol, but when some others arrived, was unable to defend his position, he avoided being captured.

He ran to Pillìs on the hill, headed to Mount Dicheo hoping for salvation. His twenty years and the fear of being taken by the enemy allowed him to sustain an effort he was not used to. Difficulty came to him when he had to descend to the sea due to the mountainous slope which was very steep. Certainly it was not an obstacle to block him; now moving away from the battle areas, he felt secure himself but he did not slow down. At sunset, he managed to reach the shore where he found other soldiers who had his own idea: to seek a boat to reach Turkey, only a few miles away, where he could find salvation.

Severino and three compatriots tried to build a raft using the trunks they found around them, and their pants belts. When they put it into the water, they realized it could bear only the weight of three of them. Severino, was reluctant to escape; he preferred to be taken prisoner. *"What else could happen to me,"* he thought bitterly; but, later, with hindsight he added *"I could have asked for a Greek family's asylum in return for labour."*

The next morning, tired and hungry, he set off on the steep slope of the mountain to return to Pillis: he wanted to hand himself as a prisoner to the Germans.

By sunset he came to a deserted village. Severino walked with caution. He went on slowly for his tiredness and for fear of being subjected to gunshots.

He met a young boy, Stelios Kourounis, to whom he asked in his language something to eat. He walked away to his home without making a sign. Severino waited with the hope that the boy would come back, but a German patrol saw and caught him. At first he was brought to their command and questioned.

Then he was accompanied into the village's orthodox church. He had lost hopes of getting something to eat when, as he was about to enter the church, that boy and a woman approached him. Despite the guards' reaction, she handed him a loaf of bread that he shared with other prisoners being *"careful not to waste a crumb "*

The following day, the prisoners were transferred from Pillis to the Antimachia sports field, a 16 km ride, where they received a piece of black bread. Then they were forced to work on the landing ground to repair the damage caused by air bombardment.

Telling his story Severino has maintained a calm attitude. *"Now, after sixty years, it's easy to talk about those facts, but then ..."* he said and on his face I noticed disappointment only when he thought he was putting in bad light those compatriots who worked hard as prisoners or pointed to the humble jobs that together with others he was forced to do. However, the long time which has passed allows him to talk with indifference and without liveliness.

When he talks about the day he embarked on the French ship Ville d'Orange, on July 10, 1945, to be repatriated, his gaze became melancholy, thinking of how all of them, the Aegean veterans, were welcomed back in Italy.

"Entering into the Mar Grande, in Taranto, the commotion mixed with euphoria pervaded us." Severino continues. *"After three years, we finally came home. When the ship slipped into the canal with the swinging bridge, people from the seafront began to whistle, scream, call us fascists, launch tomatoes, and anything else that could hurt us morally. "*

We were not able to understand that behaviour. We caught sight of it when the ship berthed at the pier and we landed. There were Indian soldiers who forced us to get on their trucks to move us to a prison camp outside the Mar Piccolo, up the hill: Sant'Andrea camp. We then knew that in that centre, enclosed with barbed wire and cheval-de-frise, controlled by sentries, there were fascists and X Mas'Marò (marines)[32]

---

[32] http://galeso.blogspot.com/2008/01/il-nostro-campo-di-concentramento.html

Prof. Gianluca Lovreglio, *Sulle sponde del Galeso*, domenica 27 gennaio 2008: «*waiting for them there was a new concentration camp, where they were forced to wait for liberation for a few more months. The Taranto captive camps, which had been protected since the last months of 1945 by the Allied Command, hosted some ten thousand prisoners of war, forced to live in tantalizing tents and on the damp soil of the Ionian countryside.*

There we were interrogated by British officers. They asked us what we had done after September 8, 1943. With my German card, the papier, I could show that I was a forced worker. They seperated me from the others who instead had joined the German Army. These, for punishment, were dispatched to Algeria at Camp 311 where they stayed another seven months before returning definitively to Italy.

After a couple of days I was transferred to the camp of Santa Teresa, in a pine forest east of Taranto, to San Giorgio. We were free to circulate, there were no cross-links. I stayed a little. On August 2, 1945, I finally returned to Fiuggi by train.

Sixty-six years later, Severino, in 2005, felt the need to return to the island to revisit places where he had enjoyed happy and tragic moments with his compatriots and prisoners.

He went alone, to the adventure. His story is quite exciting:

In a Cos's hotel there were some Italians in charge of preparing a photographic service on the island for a travel agency. We got to know and the talk fell on the motive of my visit; so I told my story.

One of them seemed more interested than the others and offered to accompany me. We went to Pillis. I recognised the church, the German Command housing. I remembered everything: the run to Mount Dicheous for salvation and my return of despair. There I knocked at a door and an old lady, dressed in black came. I asked her how to reach the thermal spring on the mountain. I was curious to find it again. Perhaps she could not understand my speaking stunted Greek; she called a good-looking young woman who showed the way. Along the walk, I was so excited about touching the soil that I could not stop talking. I told her about the circumstances I had experienced many years before in that area. She showed much interest and made me so pleased

When we left, I thought my visit was over; instead, in the evening, a journalist came for an interview in the hotel; he had been contacted by the girl who had brought me to the source. He wanted to know all my past on

---

In particular, the "S" Field was subdivided into ten large enclosures called "Pen" (hen house), and surrounded externally by a double barbed wire fence. There was a walk between the two networks, where families of good-hearted tarantines often ventured to launch, besides the fence, food and clothing that might be comforting those heavily tried men. The Ionic population has spent a great deal to counteract this absurd situation with solidarity [...] ».

the island and by car we went to see the places familiar to me. We found the house used as a depot and for my squad accomodation, and so forth. I also pointed out those places which were inaccessible because they were Greek units' settlements. After a few days the article was published whilst I had already returned to Italy.

I was invested with a sentiment of joy and sorrow for revisiting places where I felt so much pain, and from which, unlike others, I came out fortunately. My memory went to the many friends who, perhaps less lucky than me, could not overcome the difficulties of the moment.

One day I had a phone call from Cos. It was Stelios' son, Kostas, he had learned from the newspapers the story and imagining the sense of gratitude linking me to his father for that unforgettable gesture of generous fraternal humanity, and the pleasure he would have had if he was still alive, invited me to return to the island at his own expense. I accepted in good faith. I went back to the island. Kostas was waiting for me at the airport. We hugged; the emotion was great. It was still alive in me those sad moments although very often we allow a veil to fall on the bad memories rather than on the good offers received.

What happened then was all a surprise. There were demonstrations in my honour of great sentiment at Pillis and Cardamena. I was given remembrance medals; I was interviewed by television and met people of concern who, as a simple soldier, made me feel a hero.

On that occasion, we remembered the execution of the Italian officers who I only had information about when I returned to Italy in 1945. At the Catholic cemetery I saw for the first time the Memorial tombstone with the inscriptions of the 103 officers' names, including my Lieutenant Michele D'Amore.

In the name of Stelios I promised that, age permitting, I would have made my return to Cos.

η ΠΑΓΚΩΑΚΗ

ΕΒΔΟΜΑΔΙΑΙΑ ΔΩΔΕΚΑΝΗΣΙΑΚΗ ΕΦΗΜΕΡΙΔΑ

e-mail:
pagoaki@
otenet.gr

1945-2005 ΑΦΙΕΡΩΜΑ ΣΤΑ 60 ΧΡΟΝΙΑ ΑΠΟ ΤΗ ΛΗΞΗ ΤΟΥ Β' ΠΑΓΚΟΣΜΙΟΥ ΠΟΛΕΜΟΥ

ΜΙΑ ΣΥΝΤΑΡΑΚΤΙΚΗ ΙΣΤΟΡΙΑ

ΙΤΑΛΟΣ ΣΤΡΑΤΙΩΤΗΣ ΠΟΥ ΠΟΛΕΜΗΣΕ ΣΤΗΝ ΚΩ ΗΡΘΕ ΜΕΤΑ 60 ΧΡΟΝΙΑ ΝΑ ΦΙΛΗΣΕΙ ΤΑ ΒΟΥΝΑ ΤΟΥ ΑΜΑΝΙΟΥ ΔΙΗΓΕΙΤΑΙ ΚΙ ΑΝΑΦΕΡΕΙ ΓΝΩΣΤΑ ΟΝΟΜΑΤΑ ΚΑΙ ΓΕΓΟΝΟΤΑ

" ...... στις 3 Οκτωβρίου 1943 ο αξιωματικός μου Michelle D'Amore ήταν άρρωστος στο κρεβάτι. Μια μέρα πριν, οι Γερμανοί είχαν χτυπήσει με αεροπλάνο την Κω, όπως και άλλες φορές. Αυτό το πρωί (3 . 10. 1943) είδα την απόβαση των γερμανών. Τρέχω στον αξιωματικό μου. "Διοικητά οι Γερμανοί. Έρχονται οι Γερμανοί".

"Δεν το πιστεύω" κάνει εκείνος. "Μήπως είναι δικοί μας σύμμαχοι;".

Του λέω "είναι Γερμανοί, έρχονται κατά πάνω μας",

" Πόλεμος, να πολεμήσουμε τότε" είπε εκείνος, αν και άρρωστος στο κρεβάτι και ανάψαμε πυρ "...

ΤΟ ΑΦΙΕΡΩΜΑ ΣΕΛ 8 & 9

Ο 82άχρονος σήμερα Ιταλός Soverio de Prosperis

Pagoaki (The Gazette of Cos)
A Dramatic Story
An Italian soldier fighting in Cos returned after 60 years to "kiss" the mountains of Amaniou. Tells and reports names and facts.

The Medal for the Freedom

REMEMBERING THE PAST ITALIAN TRAGEDY
KEPHALONIA AND COS

«Unlike Kephalonia, where the "Red Lodge – Casa Rossa" has become the symbol of the "Acqui" Division's heroism and focus of continuous pilgrimages, on Cos - beyond the narrow range of the Aegean's veterans - seems that a forgetfulness and indifferent veil has been stretched over the past years. Yet, in this case, we deal with valiant men who have interpreted, perhaps even more autonomously than their unfortunate colleagues of the Acqui Division, the role of their duty as commanders, and confronted tremendous consequences they were facing in resisting the Germans».

This observation appears on pag. 405 of the volume "The military Italian resistance in the Aegean Islands"

Kephalonia, the Veteran's Association [33]

A magistrate in Genoa, father of Lieutenant Lelio Triolo shot at Kefalonia, loudly promoted denouncing 28 Italian officers. The Military Attorney in Rome opened the investigation against the Italians - accused of conspiracy and rebellion against General Antonio Gandin who, according to the indictment, were induced to battle against his intentions, also against 30 German soldiers accused of murdering war prisoners. On July 8, 1957, the 28 Italians were absolved recognizing that their incitement to resistance did not constitute a crime or influenced Gandin. The trial continued for the Germans until June 14, 1960 with an absolution judgment.

The first President of the Italian Republic to visit Cephalonia was Mr. Sandro Pertini on November 22, 1980, followed by President Carlo Azeglio Ciampi on March 1, 2001. In his speech, among other things, he said: *«Their conscious choice was the first act of Italy free from Fascism Resistance».*

On April 25, 2007, President Giorgio Napolitano celebrated the 63rd anniversary of the massacre at the Monument to the Fallen to Kefalonia, present was his Greek counterpart, Mr. Karolos Papoulias.

---

[33] See: Lost Sons Of The Mediterranean – Kefalonia – September 1943: Pietro Giovanni Liuzzi author. Editor: youcanprint self-publishing - Italia

On two occasions the former Italian Minister of Defence, the actual President, Mr. Sergio Mattarella, went to the Ionian island: 28 September 2000 and 1 March 2001.

The broadcast of a little value historical movie *"Captain Corelli's Mandolin"*, by Karl Madden, inspired by Louis De Bernieres' novel, greatly influenced the acquaintance of the Acqui Division story. So did a telefiction by Riccardo Milani, *"The Cephalonia's excide"* although crammed with some historical mistakes.

The Acqui Association, Kefalonian's veterans, has strengthened since a large number of survivors, played a major role in maintaining the memory of their Division through commemorative ceremonies and rallies on the island in front of the "Fossa - the Hollow [34]" and the Monument to the Fallen and in various Italian towns. In addition, books by survivors and memories transcribed by relatives, and lectures in schools has been and still have allowed those sad events' memory to be recalled.

In the beginning the association was very numerous but, unfortunately, day by day, it declines. However, the veterans' relatives continue their activities with the support of ANPI, the Italian National Partisans Association, who has put its hands on that story.

Cos, the Aegean Veteran's Assosiation

Strangely enough, none of Cos' veterans, officers or subordinates, have had the idea of creating an associative group to write the story of what happened on that island. Except for a long and bright article

---

[34] On October 24, two days after the Acqui Division's surrender, the Italian Army officers shot at several spots in nearby camps by the Germans, were massed in the Fossa and burnt to hide the sad exsecutors' misdemeanour. Because the flames did not eliminate all trace, the bodies were carried to the shore by Italian-driven trucks. On the beach there were eight Italian sailors waiting. They were forced to load the bodies on a boat later sunk in the sea far from the coast. The eight sailors, saddened by what they were forced to do, did not want to eat what was offered to them by the German guards. These waited patiently even trying to fraternize and when it appeared the situation was finally calm, they ordered the sailors to dig holes into the sand in which they were executed and buried.

by Cosimo Taberini[35] nothing else has been reported to the public. It was necessary to wait until 1966 for some news about Cos when the *"Wardrobe of Shame"* was found.

The Aegean Veteran Association (ARDE), founded on September 20, 1968, based in Parma, has been active in the following years with its 400 members to *"consolidate brotherhood constraints, implement concrete forms of assistance for the members in need, honour the Fallen and defend the national moral virtues"*. The association, now dissolved, had a philanthropic character, out of any form of political and party ideology.

One of its activities was to push the relevant Italian Authority to search for 37 missing Italian officers. In fact, as already written, the Officers allegedly killed by the Germans were 103 and 66 of them were found in eight common pits in 1945. No Institutional Italian Authority has ever been interested in searching for them, arguing the lack of certain topographic data to address such an activity

There have been many commemorations in Italian towns and gatherings in Aegean; there was a celebratory event in Bari in 1992 held in the Overseas Military Cemetery in the presence of civilian, military, and family members of the Fallen.

The monument to the Fall of Cos was one of their initiatives. The masterpiece, designed by architects, Antonio Barrile and Dimitris Milonas, was erected in 1992 and inaugurated on October 11 in the presence of Association's and the Municipality of Cos representatives. The Mayor, Mr. Kostas Kaiserlis, said in his address:

"The people of Cos for many years has experienced and lived the fascism colonial policy however, it has been able to judge, estimate and honour the Righteous. The sacrifice of young Italian officers has created a strong bond among the Greeks, especially the ones of Cos, and the Italian people. This small monument, dedicated to them, is a sign and an example of centuries-old estimate for all the fallen in war and a message for friendship, peace and democracy addressed not only to our peoples but to the whole world."

The ARDE did dissolve because of the age of associates. The words of Carlo Berveglieri concludes this way in his book: "The

---

[35] Published in 1945 in " Reduce" The Prisoner War Survivors Association bulletin printed in Brindisi (Apulia)

Aegean, its voices": *We have done our part by placing tombstones, monuments, steles, symbols, cippus and road nameplates to leave merciful but not rhetorical traces of Men who disappeared in war. Now we need to rest and think looking for what's still not here. Our time is going to an end, and serenely - as for a fulfilled duty - we should feel content.*

The story of ARDE ended on December 16, 2000 but has taken on another role with other young people whose activity emerged after the publication in 2008 of the book "Kos, a forgotten tragedy - September 1943, May 45" [36]. The book was intended to bring out the tragic episode which occurred in Cos in 1943 to attract the attention of the institutions and possibly of the media. It was not meant to be an essay for scholars or historians.

The text, though crude in its form, has strengthened the attention of so many Italians, both at the private and institutional level, giving honour to those who sacrificed in silence their lives for loyalty not to a regime that had deceived the Italians, but for an ideal whose roots come from the Italian Risorgimento. In 2011 the book has taken on a different look with the publication of its second edition.

Cos, the Fallen of Cos Committee

Since mid-2005, the group has devoted its attention to five areas of actions: **make known** the tragedy of Cos through conferences and press articles; **raise the sacrifice** of Cos' officers to the same reputation as Kephalonia, Sant'Anna of Stazzema and others cruel events; **include Cos** in the memory itineraries (El Alamein, Kefalonia); **name public places** (roads, streets, squares, buildings etc.) to maintain memory of the Cos' victims; **find the 37 bodies** of the missing officers.

The Committee required the support of important Italian personalities. One of the so called "ensign" was the former President of the Italian Republic, Onorable Carlo Azeglio Ciampi.

---

[36] "Kos, a forgotten tragedy - September 1943, May 45" by Pietro Giovanni Liuzzi 1st edition 2008, - Edit@ -Taranto; 2nd edition 2011 – Aracne - Roma

This activity continued with more enthusiasm establishing the Committee in 2011[37]. There have been many lectures in schools and in public places in several towns; one took place in England, Durham, in the Durham Brigade Museum.

President Napolitano invited the Cos' Fallen families to the Quirinale on April 25, 2014 (during the celebration of the freedom of Italy). On that occasion his speech was focused on the long-neglected admission of that tragic episode and on the burden the families had to bear on their own. The following year, on the same National Day, President Mattarella, in mentioning the Italian venues of the Nazis's killings, included Cos too.

The ceremonies organized almost yearly by the Committee in the Catholic Cemetery of Cos have had the presence of Italian citizens, many arrived for the occasion, and foreign tourists. The participation of Cos authorities and citizens have made palpable their friendship.

The Italian Institution has been represented in all celebrations by the Military Defence Attachè at the Italian Embassy in Athens.

Nontheless, the Committee still hopes for the presence of a high rank Italian Institutions representative who, in religious silence, bends his or her head in the Campo delle Fosse (the Graves' Field) and in front of the Ossary at the Chatolic Cemetery in Cos.

---

[37] Organized by the author of this book, nominated since President of the Committee.

LYSIAS' OPERATION

In 2015 the decision to organize a weekly campaign for excavation into the Grave's Field in Linopoti - Cos to search for the bodies of the missing 37 Italian officers came up. Such an idea could be made possible having received the precious assistance of the Italian Embassy in Athens in obtaining in a short time the relevant Greek Authoritie's approval for the conduct of an excavation. Then the difficult action in collecting the necessary amount of money for the complex activity arose.

The mission was designated "Lysia's Operation" in honour of Lysia, the Athenian Jurist who, in his epitaph for the Corinthian, stated: [...] *what reasoning or time space, and what an orator would be enough to remember the value of the men who rest here [...]*

The object of the search was to find three tombs of the eleven mentioned in Father Bacheca' relation and confirmed by Lieutenant Zucchelli's report in the Grave's Field as follows [...] *There were altogether 8 tombs explored, 10 or 11 that had been definitively and on the whole pointed out. The bad weather, the disastrous condition of the soil as per vegetation and its marshy nature, made impossible the further research which were done for several days by Aiello, Avallone, Sportoletti and Gianazzi*[38], *until the sudden German order to suspend any operation concerning "those Italians' pigs". For that reason, any other tomb were, and are still, unexplored. [...]*

The operation [39], carried out from 1 to 8 July 2015, did not take place under a good omen. The situation in Greece, in that particular week, was so critical that it didn't make possible to use, except for a short time, the equipment made available by Cos Municipality for lack of fuel supply.

---

[38] Aiello was an Infantry Lieutenant. He drew the plan of the Graves' Field showing the positions of the graves, Avallone a doctor, Sportoletti a chaplain and Gianazzi a Navy Officer tasked by the German Commandant of the island to take care of the civilians' administration during their occupation.

[39] See: Operazione Lisia – Alla ricerca degli Ufficiali italiani Caduti a Kos, 6 ottobre 1943–Pietro Giovanni Liuzzi, author and Lieta Zanatta, collaborator; editor: youcanprint self-publishing – Italia - 2016.

Greek friends have contributed to the gathering of important results participating in the activity of the group of four Italian volunteers, *the musketeers*, who had omitted work and families to engage themselves in an activity of great moral value.

Despite the difficulties, the operation has been successful. Expectations were surely better, but there were historical confirmations that could open the door to the continuation of searches with greater economic and time availability on the part of those who might or should be interested.

In fact, at least one of the three tombs was identified and it is confirmed by the quantity of objects found. They were left in custody at the Cos Town Municipality for them to be exhibited in the World War II Museum opened on 7 March 2016 by the President of the Hellenic Republic, Mr. Prokopīs Paulopoulos. The bone findings, few indeed, after being tested by the Paleo-radiology laboratory at Trieste University, returned to Cos, and temporarily entombed in the Agnus Dei Church at the Catholic Cemetery wrapped in a tricolor flag.

"The Four Musketeers" at work

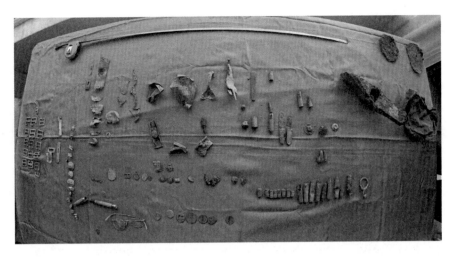

Found inventory list

Backpack Buckles	16
Hook	1
Metal Parts Belt Ends	2
Jacket artillery buttons	3 + ½
artillerymen pocket jacket buttons	4
pocket knives	4
Metallic pip star	4
Bakelite fountain pen with 3 golden rings	1
Gold Medal with the Virgin of Pompeii	1
Eyeglasses with one lens broken and other missing	1
Indistinct aluminum parts	10
Indistinct metal label	1
Little chain for Army bottle cap	several
Watch strap buckle	1
Silver Medal	1
Aluminum medal	1
Gold Medal	1
Coins 7 (one Byzantine, Greek, Turkish, two Italians, three unidentifiable)	
Silver twin elements	2
Indistinct metal parts	5
Aluminum cutlery	2
Pistol firing pin	1
Luger pistol shell casing	8
German rifle shell casing	9
Unexploded Cartridges	2
Pistol shell casing	3
Indistinct metal parts	3
Pocket knife elements	2
Ring hook	1
Pickaxe (only metal part)	1
Crushed mess tin	1
Machine gun support	2
Two teeth gold prosthesis	1

Bone findings are not shown in the photo or included in the list. They are the subject of the Paleo-radiology Institute of Trieste report

167

THE OSSUARY

The venerability of the Italian Catholic cemetery at Cos now gains more significance with the setting up of the Ossuary designed by engineers Cristiano Noce and Martino Sanna, built in its constituent elements at Locorotondo, Bari, by the Cava Calella firm and shipped to Cos to be mounted by Greek skilled specialists.

Resources were found among relatives and friends of the Officers as well as donors not directly linked to the Fallen for its realization. The pastor, Friar Luke Gregory, contributed, on behalf of the Catholic Church of Rhodes, with a substantial offer. To him goes also the merit to have given the push for the project to become reality. The collaboration of professor Jannis Trikilis, once again appreciated, arranged the activities to run smoothly.

The inauguration ceremony of the Urn and the interment of the officers remains found in Ciflica, Linopoti, in July 2015 took place exactly two years later: July 2, 2017. The representatives of Cos Municipality, the Defence Attaché on behalf of the Italian Ambassador in Athens, the president of the Veterans Association of the island, Italian and foreign guests, as well as numerous Greek friends were in attendance.

The Mayor of Cos, Mr Georgios Kiritsis, in his message said: *"The sacred land of Kos embraces and hosts the bodies of the Italian officers slain by the Nazis in October 1943. The same goes for the people of Cos preserving in their souls and memory feelings of respect and compassion for the sacrifice of those men. The people of Cos and I personally will always be present in every Memorial ceremony so required by our culture and civilization as to observe Lysia's words and the examples of our ancestors in paying respect and honour that generous men deserve.*

The Italian Ambassador in Athens, Doctor Efisio Luigi Marras, addressed these words to the attendees : *Not being able to attend today's ceremony, I entrust these words to the Defence Attachè, Colonel Frasson, to bring my greetings to the Authorities and to the guests attending the ceremony who, with their presence, keep alive the Memory of the Fallen of the Regiment Regina.*

Due to the personal commitment of Colonel Liuzzi and Father Luke the Remnants of the unknown Officers will finally find a proper place. To them go my personal and the Italian Republic's thanks.
I join you and with you I bow to the honour of our compatriots in the comfort for them to be welcomed in a friendly land.

The President of the Committee, Colonel (Rtd) Pietro Giovanni Liuzzi, concluded saying: " *The few remains of two 26-year-old Regiment Regina Officers, found in the Graves' Field in July 2015, finally receive a worthy home. This is due, if not primarily, to Father Luca who pushed me to carry on the realization of the project. I am grateful to him and to the many people who have shared this path with me today.*

Today ends the long period of my personal activity for the Fallen of Cos; I hope that someone will want to continue and ensure the Committee could continue to play its role: to keep the memory of those young people alive and stimulate the Institutions of our countries, Italy and Greece, to tighten more and more close friendship ties in the name of those who fell in the name of a shared freedom.

What was to be done has been completed. Whatever should be done is up to the Institutions.

This, of course, is not only a personal satisfaction, I would be hypocritical to deny it, but it is the tangible sign of the passionate work of those who have worked with me in the years, Italians and Greeks, and more recently to those who participated in the research and excavation. My thanks to all of them.

On the front of the Urn, it is written: "AND THEIR MEMORY IS AGELESS" *The years will pass, the people will change, but there will always be someone who, in front of this Urn, will feel called to reflect, remember, and even forgive, because this must bring us the History.*

Local television, Δημοτική TB Κος has recorded the event[40]

Three initial and the final bell's tolling dictated the time of the ceremony. A Greek soldier, on leave, offered voluntarily to play "The Last Post".

---

[40] You Tube: youtube.com/watch?v=CAhsFVfe8fQ&feature=youtu.be

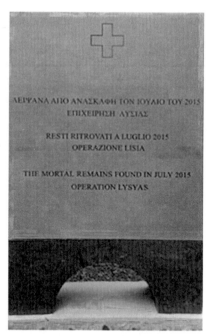

Front and backside of the Ossuary

10th Regiment Infantry "Regina" Officers' Shrine at Cos

IN MEMORY OF THE 103 ITALIAN ARMY OFFICERS

Ernesto Benzi's [41] speech at the opening of the Fallen Monument
at the Catholic Cemetery - Cos.

It was not even an act of retaliation, one of those barbaric rites asking for blood to blood, a Nibelungen atonement after the offence brought merciless Teutonic Forest gods.

It was pure and simple ferocity.

And in those tepid Greek Autumn days, when it would have been easier to throw away the arms than to put them on and save their one lives bending to the passing winner, the hundred of Cos consciously chose to sacrifice themselves as long as the Italian soldier's honour emerged bright and unharmed from the darkness of the moment.

The moral persecutors' misery offered them a glorious halo. Resistants before the Resistance took over the titles of the last national Risorgimento, first among the first and with the privilege of having preferred the idea of the Country, openly, face to face, to party ideology, they made bigger the story that had to attained People dimension.

Be glory to them.

Be glory to the Aegean soldiers of all the fighting Arms numbering almost 15,000 have not returned home from the islands. The few resting here, known, ignored or ignored by the general public that owe so much to them, are the symbol.

For them, on this day, devoted solely to Aegean memoirs, rise the souls and banners. Present Arms and play, persuasive and sweetly, the Last Post.

The neglected heroes of Cos, whose distracted history had so far been forgotten, finally in the native land peace, from the Arms' Brothers meditation have a proud and touching tribute.

---

[41] Late chairman of the Aegean Veteran Association

CONCLUSION

My reason in writing the book was to shed light on a shameful episode in wartime history in which the relative war crimes have gone unpunished and the perpetrators walk free leaving the families of the murdered Men to grieve in torment in the intervening years.

"These godless people must be made accountable" are the words marked in a very clear hand writing in the Acqui Division Museum visitors' book at Argostoli – Kefalonia. That has been for many years up to now the urgent motivation to obtain justice.

Various attempts were made after the War to bring private prosecutions against those who participated in these atrocities; most of these involving officers who were executed on Kefalonia. Individual German Officers were indicted and arraigned in legal cases in Germany, Austria and Italy; all of them collapsing under mountains of paperwork and interminable legal wrangling. It seems that the 50 Year Statute, established at Nuremburg, cannot be circumvented. These Men seem destined never to receive the Justice that they deserve.

As nascent Allies, conjoined in the same struggle, the Durham and the Italian boys fought as well as they could against a common enemy who had superiority in men and resources. In some of the engagements they fought together and gave a good account of themselves.

A friend of mine, David Wright, had the honour of knowing Captain Jack Thorpe who commanded "D" Company at Antimachia. Speaking in the late 70's, not long before he died, Jack told David: "*The Italian Lads fought as well as we did on that island. The whole show was doomed to failure.*"

The morale of the Italian troops was poor before the Germans came to Cos. They spent their time in indolence, worrying about their families back home and how long they would have to garrison the island before they ever saw them again.

The arrival of the British was a boost to their morale, but was short –lived because the British were cold and hostile viewing the Italians with suspicion. The amount of materiel and equipment pouring into

Cos by planes gave the Italians the impression that behind those troops there were all the Forces of the Middle East.

The British efficiency in putting in order the landing strip at Antimachia airport and the rapidity in organizing a second airport at Lambi gave confidence to the Italians. But, when, at the end of the first day of battle, the news spread out that the British troops were leaving Cos for Turkey, created a lot of fear and uncertainty.

The invasion of Cos led to a quick defeat of the Italian - British troops: the first were garrison troops carrying out formal barracks training and shooting exercises during which they would shoot one or two '91 musket cartridges. In addition, many soldiers were tired of the long stay on the island without having been on leave to see their families for a while. Some had spent seven years in service. The other, the British troops, in the last two years had been employed on Malta to get rid of the debris or repair the damages caused by German air raids. To catch up with some military training, before being transferred to Cos, they had to carry out a period of 15 days of exercises in the Egyptian desert.

On the other hand, it must not be neglected the lack of understanding among the British-Italian Commanding Officers and poor, if not absent, cooperation among troops. Intelligence Service's was highly ineffective for the whole period.

In 36 hours the Italians and the British forces had to surrender.

There was strong disparities in the aviation, military training, equipment and, perhaps more importantly, discipline.

A Kefalonian veteran a few days earlier (September 15 to 22) went through what was happening in those days on Cos. He was amazed to see landing Germans equipment never seen before. One of them suddenly attracted his eyes: it was a field mobile kitchen. Empty oil bins were used for cooking the unit meals in his garrison, reported in a talk.

200 German planes were detached from the Russian front to the one in Aegean. They were painted white, as an English officer reports, to throw the enemy in confusion in a snowy landscapes.

The German troops were trained, having taken part in the Eastern and/or central European fronts; accustomed to the Prevertin drug [42] and equipped with the most modern armament. Just think of the MG 42 machine gun (Maschinengewehr 42), which has been in service in the NATO Armies until the '90s, although appropriately improved in '59.

MG 42 - Mauser - production year 1942 – Rate of fire: 1.200 / 1.550 per minute - allowed 250 per minute due to barrel overheating - range 1.500 m – caliber 8 mm

Breda 37 - production year 1937 – Rate of fire 450 / min. - defect: jamming caused by the loading of the bullet clip (sand, imprecise loading of the clip or erroneous loading of the bullet in the clip) - range: 1.000 m – caliber: 8 mm.

At the end of the fighting, against the losses of numerous paratroopers hit by the Italian weapons while descending, General

---

[42] Allucinogen that gave courage and prolonged physical efforts

Müller was able to communicate to the high command a substantial list of materials and equipment requisites in addition to the number of prisoners: about 3,000 Italians and a thousand Englishmen (including aggregate Indians employed for the construction of the landing strips).

In fact, the German troops put their hands on large quantities of ammunition, fuel and food, eleven efficient planes (7 South African Spitfires and 4 Macchi fighters), 40 artillery guns of 75 and 149 mm calibre, 16 antiaircraft weapons of 20 and 40 mm calibre.

Strategic action was superb. The human acrimony is still considered totally detestable.

A General consideration

An historian should tell the facts as they are without personal opinion and or from the moment's orientations; I personally feel that I have reported the events on Cos by cross checking information wherever possible. For the sake of the truth, I have to indicate two facts which have disturbed me because they put the adversaries in bad light.

- The DLI English Major K.M.W. Leather, during the period spent in Germany at the Oflag VIII F camp in Brunswick, wrote a memorial in which he expresses a very harsh judgment on the behaviour of the Italians during the fighting at Marmari at Cos on October 3, 1943. It is an unfair, unilateral and ungenerous judgment because it was limited to what he saw but in contrast to what others reported.

Anthony Rogers, in his book, "Churchill's Folly" writes: "[...] *Their opponents, whoever they were, were resolute and brave men* [...]" and reports a statement by Major Hugh Vaux, pro tempore DLI Commanding Officer :"*The two Italian companies fought well; in fact they kept their position until sunset, although there were enemy infiltrations on their left side.*"

- Vice-Admiral Commander in Chief A.U. Willis in his report (see

Page 103 paras 10 & 11) writes *"stubborn resistance from the British battalion, who received small assistance from the Italian garrison"* and " *the Italians' attitude was co-operative in the islands visited by us, though their fighting value was low."*

The following assertions have been copied from the Abstention report[43]:

"The events of the battle for Castellorizo during Operation Abstention (25 – 28 February 1941) remain practically unknown, even for many scholars of World War Two. Information and accounts of the operation are scarce, and are often reduced to a footnote or blurb, if in fact mentioned at all in Western coverage of the War. There are several reasons for this including; the relatively small size of the forces involved in the fighting, the initial limited nature of the operation, the peripheral positioning of the combat area, and western writers' proclivity to focus subject matter almost exclusively on the Western Allies and or German forces." and *"The failure of Operation Abstention came as a complete surprise to the British. Churchill's dreams of Allied unity and power in the Aegean were dashed before they even started. The shocked Prime Minister stated in disbelief "I am thoroughly mystified at this operation." Even the genius of Admiral Cunningham had not counted upon the Italians dealing his forces a loss in this endeavor; "A rotten business" is how the Admiral would refer to it during a post analysis of the operation. Writer Vincent O'Hare assigned the blame of Abstention's failure on the British's tendency to underestimate their Italian foe, and summarized "...It would not be the last time the British suffered embarrassment in an operation where success depended upon a lack of Italian initiative."*

There is an Italian movie "Mediterraneo" which show, as a fiction with comic reflections and for this quite tragic, how the small garrison of Castellorizo spent their '40 early years on that island. It was made up with a tiny group of soldiers and agents of the Guardia di Finanza (Custom Service) poorly dressed, badly armed, unwilling to work, to fight, who responded, as it really happened, to the attacks of the

---

[43] http://www.comandosupremo.com/operation-abstention-the-battle-for-castellorizo-25-28-february-1941.html

British special forces. This happened on more than one occasion before the 8th September 1943 Armistice.

I thought long and hard for a suitable ending to this my work and I am drawn to Thucydides' funeral oration for Pericles, which neatly summarizes my feeling on the matter:

> *"The whole earth is the tomb of heroic men,*
> *And their story is not only inscribed on stone over their graves,*
> *But abides everywhere, without visible symbol,*
> *Woven into the stuff of other men's lives...."*

ANNEXES

10th Infantry Regiment "Regina"
motto
"Sicut Te Candidi Candidissima Regina"
Candid like you, candid Queen

It originates from the battalion "The Queen" constituted in Pinerolo on April 8, 1734 by Count Cacherano of Bricherasio. Released in 1798 by the oath of fidelity to the King of Sardinia, it was re-established in 1814 as the "Regina". It changes over time the denomination and on March 11, 1926 becomes the 10th Infantry regiment "Regina" comprising two battalions.

It is part of the 23rd Infantry Brigade along with the 9th Regina and 47th

"Ferrara" until its transfer to the Aegean on July 5, 1938, where it becomes part of the Fifth Infantry Division "Regina" with the 9th, 309th and the 50th artillery regiments as an infantry division.

In June 1940 the regiment was reformed comprising Command Headquarters, 1st, 2nd and 3rd infantry battalions, 81mm Mortar Company, battery of accompanying weapons of 65/17.

The Command Headquarters with the 1st and 2nd battalions were located on Cos where they were defeated on October 4, 1943; the 3rd battalion was stationed at Lero where it fought until November 16 of the same year when they had to surrender to the Germans.

Regimental Honours and Awards derive from the actions carried out in World War I and are: Italian military order, two gold medals, one silver medal and two bronze medals.

Its last posting before transferring to the Aegean was Bari where it remained from 1908 to 1937.

The rectangular gorget patch is coloured white.

The Regiment anniversary is the 29th June, the recurrence of the fight at Bosco Cappuccio (1916).

The Regiment war cry: "**The white**"

Commander in Chief of the Army in the Middle East
Address to the Greek population

Μύνημα τοῦ Ἀρχιστρατήγου
τοῦ Στρατοῦ Μέσης Ἀνατολῆς
πρὸς τὸν Ἑλληνικὸν Λαὸν

ΕΛΛΗΝΕΣ,

Οἱ Ἰταλοὶ ἐνικήθησαν καὶ ἐγονάτισαν. Ὑπέγραψαν **ἀνακωχὴν** μὲ τὰ Ἡνωμένα Ἔθνη. Ἡ γενναία δρᾶσις τῶν Ἐθνικῶν Ἀνταρτικῶν Ὁμάδων τῆς Ἑλλάδος καὶ τῶν μυστικῶν ὀργανώσεων συνετέλεσεν εἰς τὴν ἐξάρθρωσιν τῶν Ἀξονικῶν σχεδίων καὶ εἰς τὴν νίκην τῶν Συμμάχων εἰς τὴν Ἰταλίαν Οἱ Ἰταλοὶ ὑποχρεοῦνται νὰ ἐφαρμώσουν τοὺς ὅρους τῆς ἀνακωχῆς. ἄλλως ὑπόκεινται εἰς ποινὰς καὶ τιμωρίας Τὰ ἰταλικὰ στρατεύματα τώρα ὑπακούουν τὰς ἰδικάς μου διαταγὰς καὶ οὐχὶ τὰς διαταγὰς τῶν Γερμανῶν. Σύμφωνα μὲ τὰς διαταγάς μου πρέπει ἀμέσως νὰ σταματήσουν πᾶσαν ἐχθροπραξίαν ἔναντι τῶν Ἑλλήνων Τὰ πλοῖα τῶν πρέπει νὰ παραδοθοῦν εἰς τὰ Ἡνωμένα Ἔθνη Τὰ ἀεροπλάνα τους νὰ πετάξουν πρὸς Συμμαχικὰ ἀεροδρόμια. Δὲν τοὺς ἐπιτρέπεται νὰ παραδώσουν τὰ ὅπλα καὶ τὰ ἐξαρτήματα τους ἢ ὀχυρωμένας θέσεις εἰς τοὺς Γερμανούς Ὁ πόλεμος ἐξακολουθεῖ ἐναντίον τῶν Γερμανῶν, τῶν κυρίων ἐχθρῶν. οἱ ὁποῖοι προσπαθοῦν νὰ παρατείνουν τὴν σκλαβιὰ τῆς πατρίδος σας. Εἰς ὅλους τοὺς φίλους μας λέγω :

1) Μὴν ἐμποδίσετε τοὺς Ἰταλοὺς νὰ ἐπιστρέφουν εἰς τὰς σπίτια τους.

2) Οἱ Γερμανοὶ θὰ προσπαθήσουν νὰ προκαλέσουν ταραχὰς καὶ αἱματοχυσίαν μεταξὺ Ἑλλήνων καὶ Ἰταλῶν διὰ νὰ ἐνισχύσουν τὴν ἰδικήν των θέσιν. Νὰ μὴ σᾶς γελάσῃ αὐτὸ τὸ τέχνασμα.

Εἰς ἐκείνους ποὺ πολεμοῦν τοὺς Ἀξονικοὺς εἰς τὸ ὕπαιθρον λέγω: Προμηθευθῆτε ἄνευ βίας ἰταλικὰ ὅπλα καὶ πολεμεφόδια διὰ νὰ δυνηθεῖτε νὰ ἐξακολουθήσετε τὸν γενναῖον σας ἀγῶνα μὲ τὸν ἀπομένοντα ἐχθρὸν μὲ μεγαλειτέραν ἐπιτυχίαν.

Εἰς ἐκείνους ποὺ περιμένουν νὰ ἴδουν τὴν ἐξέλιξιν τῶν πραγμάτων λέγω: Ἀποφασίστε τώρα ἢ καταστραφῆτε καὶ σεῖς εἰς τὴν παγκολευθερίαν ποὺ ἀναμένει τοὺς Γερμανούς.

Εἰς τοὺς φίλους μας ποὺ δὲν ἔχουν φανερωθῆ ἀκόμη λέγω: Οἱ Γερμανοὶ θὰ προσπαθήσουν τώρα μὲ πονηρίες νὰ σᾶς ξεγελάσουν ν' ἀποκαλύψετε τὰ σχέδιά σας καὶ τὰς ὀργανώσεις σας πρόωρως. Τοιουτοτρόπως σχεδιάζουν νὰ σᾶς καταστρέψουν ἕναν-ἕναν. Μὴ γελασθῆτε Ἡ ὥρα τῆς τελικῆς ἀπελευθερώσεως πλησιάζει ἀλλὰ δὲν ἔφθασε ἀκόμη. Ἀναμένετε τὸ σύνθημα τῆς γενικῆς ἐξεγέρσεως. Ἐν τῷ μεταξὺ ἡ μάχη τῶν Ἡνωμένων Ἐθνῶν ἐναντίον τῶν Γερμανῶν ἐξακολουθεῖ. Οἱ Γερμανοὶ θὰ καταστραφοῦν τελείως.

Translation

Greeks

The Italians are losing and kneeling. They signed the armistice with the United Nations. The courageous action of nationalist partisan groups in Greece and secret organizations has contributed to the disorganization of Axis plans and the victory of allies in Italy. Italians have an obligation to apply the conditions of the armistice, otherwise they will be subjected to penalties and punishments.

The Italian Armed Forces now obey our provisions and not the orders of the Germans. According to my orders, every hostility towards the Greeks must stop immediately. Their ships must be delivered to the United Nations. Their airplanes head to allied airports. They are not allowed to deliver their weapons and related equipment or fortified posts to the Germans. The war against the Germans continues; they are the main enemies who try to prolong the slavery of your homeland. To all our friends I say:

1. Do not stop the Italians from returning to their homes.

2. The Germans will try to cause disorder and blood shedding between Greeks and Italians to strengthen their position. Do not be deceived by this cunning.

To those who fight the Axis forces in the open, I say, get yourself, without violent acts, Italian weapons and ammunition to continue your courageous struggle against the surviving enemy, with greater success.

Those who are waiting to see what developments decide now or condemn the extermination that the Germans are waiting for.

To our friends who have not yet presented, I will say: Germans will now try to deceive you with confusion as you advance your plans and organizations. They propose to destroy you one by one. Do not fall for this deceit. The time of final liberation is approaching but has not yet come. Wait for the general awakening password. Meanwhile, the United Nations battle against the Germans continues. The Germans will be completely destroyed.

Order
Commander in Chief of the Allied Forces In the Middle East to all Italian troops in the Balkans and Aegean areas

ORDINE

DEL COMANDANTE IN CAPO DELLE FORZE ALLEATE NEL MEDIO ORIENTE A TUTTE LE TRUPPE ITALIANE NELLA ZONA DEI BALCANI E DELL'EGEO

Ufficiali, sottufficiali e soldati delle Forze Armate italiane,

Il vostro Governo ha firmato l'Armistizio. La guerra fra l'Italia e le Nazioni Unite è terminata.

In conformità alle condizioni d'armistizio diramo i seguenti ordini che debbono essere immediatamente eseguiti da chiunque appartenga alle Forze Armate italiane dislocate nei Balcani e nell'Egeo:

1.-Ogni atto ostile verso le popolazioni del paese in cui vi trovate deve cessare a partire da questo momento.

2.-In tutte le unità dev'essere mantenuta la più rigida disciplina, ed ogni reparto dovrà mantenere la sua attuale formazione.

3.-Ad ogni tentativo da parte dei tedeschi o dei loro satelliti di disarmare o disperdere le forze italiane, d'impossessarsi delle loro armi, magazzini, carburanti ed acqua o dei punti in cui esse sono di guarnigione, dovrà essere opposta la massima resistenza con le armi. Non si deve tenere alcun conto di ogni ordine trasmesso dai tedeschi.

4.-Le truppe italiane del Dodecaneso assumeranno con la forza il controllo di tutti i punti ora in possesso dei tedeschi.

5.-Tutte le unità della Regia Marina e della Marina mercantile italiana salperanno immediatamente facendo la seguente rotta:

Navi mercantili che si trovano in un punto ad Est di 17° E procederanno direttamente su ALESSANDRIA. Nel solo caso sia necessario far rifornimento di carburante possono fare scalo in un porto intermedio delle Nazioni Unite.

Navi da guerra nell'Egeo, rotta diretta su CAIFA.

6.-Tutti gli aerei della Regia Aeronautica si dirigeranno immediatamente in volo verso NICOSIA, DERNA, TOBRUK (idrovolanti), EL ADEM.

Nell'avvicinarsi e nell'atterrare in territorio alleato i velivoli italiani dovranno seguire le seguenti istruzioni:

(a) Volare al largo dalla rotta di ogni nave, ed evitare i porti nell'avvicinarsi alla costa;

(b) Volare a 900 metri di quota col carrello d'atterraggio abbassato a partire da una distanza di 32 chilometri dalla costa sino al campo d'aviazione scelto per l'atterraggio.

(c) Prima d'atterrare fare due giri completi a sinistra sull'aerodromo alla quota di 300 metri.

La mancata ottemperanza al presente ordine o a quelli che saranno successivamente da me emanati sarà considerata come una violazione delle condizioni d'armistizio accettate dal vostro Comandante Supremo e pregiudicherà il vostro trattamento futuro.

firmato: generale H.M. WILSON,
Comandante in Capo
delle Forze del Medio Oriente

Translation

Officers, Non Commissioned Officers and Soldiers of the Italian Armed Forces

Your Government has signed the Armistice. The war between Italy and the United Nations has come to an end.

In accordance with the Armistice conditions we issue the following orders that must be executed immediately by anyone who belongs to the Italian Armed Forces located in the Balkans and the Aegean.

1.- Every hostile act against the peoples of the countries you are in must cease from this moment

2.- In all Units the strictest discipline must be respected and each department will have to maintain its current formation

3.- Any attempt by the Germans or their satellites to disarm or dispose of the Italian forces, to seize their weapons, warehouses, fuel and water or their garrisons must be opposed by using their weapons to provide maximum resistance. No account must be taken of any order transmitted by the Germans.

4.- The Italian troops of the Dodecanese will take over the control of all the places now possessed by the Germans

5.- All the units of the Italian Royal Navy and the Merchant Navy will sail immediately to

- merchant vessels located at a point east of 17 ° E will immediately proceed to Alexandria. Only in the case of refuelling, they might stop in an interim port of the United Nations

- Warships in the Aegean, must take a direct route to Caifa.

6. All aircraft of the Italian Royal Air Force will directly head to Nicosia, Derna, Tobruk (seaplanes), El Adem.

When approaching allied territory, the following instructions must be followed by the Italian aircraft:

(a) Flying clear of each ship and avoiding ports approaching the coast,

(b) Flying at 900 metres of altitude with the landing gear lowered from a distance of 32 kms from the coast to the aviation field chosen for landing

(c) Before landing, make two full laps left on the airplane at 300 metres.

Failure to comply with this order or those to be subsequently issued will give rise to a violation of the armistice conditions accepted by your supreme commander and will undermine your future treatment.

Signed: General H. M. Wilson

Commander in Chief Middle East Forces

SOME ITALIAN ARCHITECT'S PROJECTS
FOR AFTER EARTHQUAKE COS TOW

Prospect of Rotonda Square

Turkish fountain in Platano Square

Front sea prospect of buildings

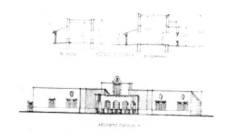

Prospect of Ippocrateus Liceum

Prospect of Infants' School

SOURCES OF RESEARCH

The National Archives - London
The British Library Newspapers - London
The Durham County Council - Durham - England
Archivio storico Parlamento italiano
Archivio Ufficio storico Stato maggiore Esercito
Archivio Ufficio storico Stato maggiore Marina
Archivio Ufficio storico Stato maggiore Aeronautica
Archivio Ufficio storico Comando generale Arma dei carabinieri
Archivio Ufficio storico Comando della guardia di finanza

PHTO SUPPLIERS

Comando Artiglieria Contraerei Esercito
Giuliano Cappelli
Soldato del Mundo , Web page
Stamos J. Papastamatiou
Imperial War Museum
Kostas Kojiopoulos
Vasilii Hatzivasilieu

BIBLIOGRAPHY

S. Bertoldi, *Badoglio*, Rizzoli, Milano, 1982.

C. Berveglieri, *L'Egeo, le sue voci*, ARDE, Milano, 1984.

L.V. Bertarelli, *Guida d'Italia del TCI, sez. Possedimenti e colonie* , Bertarelli, Milano, 1929-Anno VII.

M. Cervi, *Storia della guerra di Grecia, ottobre '40- aprile '41*, Rizzoli, Milano, 2000.

A. De Feo-F. Giustolisi, *Lasciate stare Erich il nazista*, in "L'Espresso", 22 marzo 1996.

A. De Feo- F. Giustolisi, *Una, cento, mille Ardeatine*, in "L'Espresso", 22 agosto 1996.

L. Dogliani, *Ulisse '43*, Cooperativa grafici genovesi, Genova, 1984.

B. Dradi Maraldi, R.Pieri, *Lotta armata e resistenza delle FFAA italiane all'estero*, Franco Angeli, Milano, 1990.

N. Doumanis, *Mith, and Memory in the Mediterranean, remembering fascism? Empire*, Mac Millan Press Ltd., Mac Millan, New York, 1997.

E. Fino, *La tragedia di Kos*, Edizioni Assegeo, Milano, 1963.

F. Focardi, *Un accordo segreto tra Italia e Rft sui criminali di guerra. La liberazione del "gruppo di Rodi" 1948-1951*, in "Italia Contemporanea", 232, settembre 2003, http://www.insmli.it/pubblicazioni/1/focardi_232.pdf, 31/10/10.

M. Franzinelli, *Le stragi nascoste*, Le Scie, Mondadori, 2002.

F. Giustolisi, *L'armadio della vergogna*, Nutrimenti, Roma, 2004

E. Grazzi, *Il principio della fine (L'impresa della Grecia)*. Editrice Faro, Roma, 1945.

Ist. Studi Politica Intern., *Relazioni internazionali. Settimanale di politica estera*, ISPI, 1941.

P. Juso, *La resistenza dei militari italiani all'estero. Isole dell'Egeo*, La Rivista militare, Roma, 1994.

K. Kogiopoulos, *L'armistizio italiano del 08.09.1943. L'esecuzione degli ufficiali italiani a Linopoti e il processo del generale Müller*, Koaka, Tomo V, Associazione culturale Filitas, Atene, 1995.

G. Manicone, *Italiani in Egeo*, Abbazia Casamari, Frosinone, 1989.

C. Marongiu Buonaiuti, *Politica religiosa del fascismo nel Dodecanneso*, Università di Napoli, Facoltà di scienze politiche, Napoli, 1979.

I. Palermo, *Storia di un armistizio*, Mondadori, Milano, 1967.

K.Papagiorgiou, in *Testimonianze '40-'41*, a cura di K.N. Chatzipateras e M.Fafalio, (traduzione in italiano di E. Porcelli), ed. Kedros, Atene, 1982..

L. Picciotto Fargion, *Per ignota destinazione- Gli ebrei sotto il nazismo*, Le Scie, Mondadori, Milano, 1994.

R. Pieri, G. Rochat, *Badoglio*, Unione tipografica, Torino, 1974.

Q. Reynolds, *W. Churchill-Il difensore del mondo libero*, Mursia, Milano, 1963.

G. Rochat, *Saggio sulla divisione Acqui a Cefaloni*, in "Annali del dipartimento di Storia", Università Tor Vergata, Roma, dicembre 2006.

A. Rogers, *Churchill's folly. Leros and the Aegean, The last great british defeat of the 2° World War*, Cassel military paperbook, Berkshire UK, 2003.

S. W. Roskill, *The war at sea, Vol. IIIm Part.I*, The Naval and military Press Ltd, UK, 2004.

P. Schenk, *War in the Aegean (Kamf um die Ägeäis)*, Hamburg, Mittler, 2000.

D. M. Smith, *Le guerre del duce*, Laterza, Bari, 1980.

Ufficio storico della Marina militare, *Avvenimenti in Egeo dopo l'armistizio. Rodi, Lero e le isole minori*, Roma, 1993.

P. Vaenti, *Luci nella catastrofe*, Società editrice il Ponte vecchio, Cesena, 2002.

Possedimento delle isole italiane dell'Egeo, Industrie grafiche A. Nicola & C, Varese-Milano, Giugno 1937-XV.

ITALIAN DODECANESE CHRONOLOGY

30	Mar	1911	Giolitti Government settlement
26	Nov		Ultimatum to Turkey to abandon Libya
18	Apr	1912	The Italian naval force strengthens the Dardanelles
5	May		1st Governor: Gen. Giovan Battista Ameglio,
6-20	May		Italian occupation of the Dodecanese
18	Oct		1st Lausanne treaty = end of the Italian Turkish conflict
13	Nov	1913	2nd Governor: Maj. Gen. Francesco Marchi
28	Jul	1914	Start of WWI
20	Aug		Italy declares neutrality
29	Oct		Turkey entered the war
middle	Jan	1915	Start of Turkey coasts bombardment
25	Apr		Amphibious landing on Turkey coasts
26	Apr		Pact of London = Full sovereignty of Italy in the Dodecanese
24	May		Italy entered the war
	Jan	1916	France and Great Britain withdraw from Turkey
27	Apr	1917	3rd Governor: Maj.Gen.Giovanni Croce
07	Dec		United States entered the war
4	Nov	1918	End of WW1
16	Dec	1919	4th Governor: Brig.Gen. Achille Porta
17	Sept	1920	5th Governor: Felice Maiassa
17	Aug	1921	6th Governor: Conte Alessandro De Bosdari
28	Oct	1922	March to Rome
29	Oct		Mussolini to form the government in Italy
20	Nov		7th Governor: Mario Lago
24	July	1923	2nd Lausanne treaty : (in force from August 6, 1924) Dodecanese Italian sovereignty confirmation
5-16	Oct	1925	Locarno Conference
23	Apr	1933	Cos earthquake, 0080
3	Oct	1935	Start fighting in Ethiopia
	Nov		Sanctions on Italy come into force
19	Feb	1936	8th Governor: Cesare Maria De Vecchi
15	Jun		Revocation of Sanctions to Italy
7-8	Apr	1939	Italian occupation of Albania
22	Maj		Pact of Steel Agreement signature = Italy and Germany
1	Sept		Germany invade Poland
3	Sept		France / G.B. declare war with Germany
10	Jun	1940	Italy enters war as Germany ally
10-24	Aug		Quebec Conference
14	Aug		USA – UK signature of Atlantic Charter
27	Sept		Triple Alliance : Italy Germany and Japan
28	Oct		Italy invade Greece
10	Dec		9th Governor: Marshall of Italy Ettore Bastico
middle	Jan	1941	Luftwaffe Units from Norway to Sicily
	Jan/Feb		Africa Korps in North Africa
24	Jul		10th Governor: Adm. Inigo Campioni

7	Dec		USA in war - Pearl Harbor
end	Mar	1942	Germany invade Greece
	May		Germany invade Crete
14-24	Jan	1943	Casablanca Conference
	Feb		USA landing in Africa (Casablanca, Orano, Algeri)
5	Feb		Galeazzo Ciano deposed as Foreign Affairs Minister
5	Mar		Industrial strike in North Italy
12	May		Washington Conference
12-13	May		Axis defeat in Africa
10	Jul		Allied landing in Sicily
19	Jul		Rome bombed
25	Jul		Great Council versus Mussolini – End Fascism Era
13	Aug		Rome, open city
3	Sept		Allied landing at Reggio Calabria
3	Sept		Italy signs Armistice with Allies
8	Sept		Broadcasting of the Armistice
9	Sept		British Army Officer arrives in Cos
9	Sept		Allied landing at Salerno and Taranto
9	Sept		The Italian King and his government leave Rome
13	Sept		First batch of British units at Cos
13- 22	Sept		Battle at Kefalonia
14	Sept		1st *Durham Light Infantry* arrive at Cos
23-24	Sept		Sinking of Donizetti transport ship – 1593 Italian prisoners died
3 - 4	Oct		Cos German attack
13	Oct		Badoglio declares war on Germany
18	Oct		Sinking of Sinfra transport ship = 1850 Italian prisoners died
22	Jan	1944	Allied landing at Anzio
8	Feb		Sinking of Petrella
11	Feb		Sinking of Oria (Norda 4) due to sea storm – 4.200 Italian prisoners died
06-14	Jun		Allied landing in France
4	Jun		American troops enter Rome
1	Oct		German Army leaves Athens
29	Apr	1945	German Armed Forces surrender to the Allies in Italy (in Caserta)
9	May		German Forces in Dodecanese surrender at Symi
10	Feb	1947	Paris Treaty : Dodecanese cession by Italy
31	Mar		Dodecanese to Greece
7	Mar	1948	Dodecanese integrated into Greek territory

INDEX

W

ACKNOWLEDGMENTS

I do wish to thank two of my great supporters; I appreciate the time and work they put into reviewing my texts:

- David Wright of Shotley Bridge in County Durham for allowing me to know and have access to the DLI Museum in Durham from which I have obtained many contributions. I wish to thank him for his help in editing the English version of my book *The Lost Sons of the Mediterranean*. David was greatly moved by a visit to the Acqui Division Museum in Argostoli – Kefalonia and wrote a moving tribute in the visitor's book. Subsequently we made contact and became firm friends and I have appreciated the great love he has for Kefalonia and its people.

- John Fenton for the friendship that has linked us for many years: it dates back to 1977. We met at Woolwich in London because we were lodged in the same Residence for Army Officers in Worthy Down Court, Shooters' Hill. John, Australian nationality, was serving on an exchange-basis in a British Technical Unit. In those days I participated in the role as the Italian Representative at the FH70 System Management Team. Although a few months later I had to return back to Italy our relationships continued over the time through letters; now it is easier and faster to communicate via the internet. John, now retired, undertook training becoming a volunteer Advocate to support and advise veterans with their dealings with the Australian Department of Veterans' Affairs. This volunteering role continues currently. So, though engaged, John accepted my proposal to revise my English text which has now been published and I hope to welcome readers' favours for the content and for the linearity how the facts are described.

Finito di stampare nel mese di Novembre 2017
per conto di Youcanprint *Self-Publishing*